Queer Noises

The Cassell Lesbian and Gay Studies list offers a broad-based platform to lesbian, gay and bisexual writers for the discussion of contemporary issues and for the promotion of new ideas and research.

COMMISSIONING:
Steve Cook
Roz Hopkins

CONSULTANTS:
Liz Gibbs
Keith Howes
(Australia)
Christina Ruse
Peter Tatchell

Queer Noises

Male and Female Homosexuality in Twentieth-Century Music

John Gill

CASSELL

Cassell
Villiers House
41/47 Strand
London WC2N 5JE

First published 1995

British Library Cataloguing-in-Publication Data
A catalogue record for this book is available from the British Library.

ISBN 0-304-34304-8 (hardback)
　　　0-304-34302-1 (paperback)

Typeset by Fakenham Photosetting Limited, Fakenham, Norfolk
Printed and bound in Great Britain by Mackays of Chatham

Contents

For
Johnny Mathis –
and Spud Jones

Acknowledgements

I have a debt of thanks to a number of people: Antony Grey, for proposing this project; Steve Cook for commissioning and supporting it; and John Banks for editing it.

A number of people went out of their way to assist me: among them Gary Burton, Tom Robinson, David Revill, Graham Russell, Cleo Sylvestre, and the long-suffering Graham.

I must also thank the staff of Westminster Music Library, the National Sound Archive and the British Library Newspaper Library at Colindale – three fine institutions still open and still free after 15 years of you-know-what.

Anyone who says, 'Well, I don't care if he/she is gay, it's nobody's business,' is the voice of heterosexual culture inviting gay people to be invisible. Heterosexuals have proms and weddings and anniversaries, get breaks on insurance and health care, they are all over each other on billboards, in movies and at football games. You bet it matters to them.

- Holly Near, *Fire in the Rain ... Singer in the Storm*

The only way to attack homophobia is to refuse to maintain the secret of homosexuality, either your own or anyone else's.

- Armistead Maupin, interviewed in *Au Courant* (Philadelphia)

To refuse to bring Barthes out consents to a homophobic reception of his work.

- D. A. Miller, *Bringing out Roland Barthes*

Chapter one

Pet Shop Boys, Naturally

IT was barely a squall in a teacup, but the incident could give a focus to the subject at hand. It might also measure the degree of madness, deception and irrational behaviour attending the matter. Certainly, it must be the first time a critic ever fell foul of a band for giving them a rave review.

The review in question was of *Please*, the first album by the Pet Shop Boys. It was written by me, in 1986, and appeared in the London listings magazine *Time Out*, where I was music editor at the time. Rock journalists are not meant to like each other's extra-curricular activities, particularly those that feed the myth that rock hacks are basically frustrated musicians. Former *Smash Hits* journalist Neil Tennant and accomplice Chris Lowe's duo had made an unimpressive debut at London's Institute of Contemporary Arts, and despite the appeal of 'West End Girls', Tennant and Lowe's venture bore the hallmark of outrageous hubris. There are few things that rock journalists delight in so much as savaging each other, and a fair-sized crowd had been gathering to watch the debut Pet Shop Boys album perform a monumental pratfall.

It did nothing of the sort, of course, instead garnering positive reviews throughout the media. In praising it to the skies, I commented that it knocked the likes of ABC into the bargain dumper bins and essayed a sophisticated pop elegance like no other. I also commented, without thinking, really, that it had a strong gay subtext.

When the review appeared, a press officer – also gay – at their record company reported that the duo were 'climbing the walls' because of my review. Perplexed, I mentioned this to gay friends who had gone out and bought *Please* because they thought they were buying an album by a pop group who were at least 50 per cent gay. The gay friends I asked about this, when I mentioned I was worried that I might have read a private assumption into the album, assured me that they too had picked up that selfsame subtext. Then heterosexuals started telling me they too had picked up that subtext.

There was a certain, minor, amount of history between Tennant and myself, although at the time we had not met. A woman colleague had met him at a party. Somehow, the conversation got around to 'out' gay rock journalists. Tennant informed her that there was no such beast; she told him that I was both out and a rock hack, and reported that Tennant seemed bemused by the information. In reviewing *Please*, I had simply presumed, as is indeed the case, that Tennant is a homosexual. Heterosexuals do not write songs like that, say things like that, in private or in song.

The problem, their gay publicist told me, was that Neil Tennant 'hadn't come out to his mum yet'. This is quite probable, but for the Pet Shop Boys to launch their career and imagine that this information might remain both in private and in their control seems too naive for a group who have styled themselves as clever and knowing. It is just possible that – in the way that most of us imagined, from the shadows of the closet, that no one else could spot us – Tennant and Lowe did not understand that they were sending messages, semiotic information, on *Please*. This, too, seems odd, especially for a group who have made pop semiotics so much a part of their career. And for the whole thing to revolve on the fact that Tennant 'hadn't come out to his mum' seemed almost farcical. It is almost as likely that the duo imagined, with the blithe arrogance of pop stars, fully fledged or manqué, that they could keep this information to themselves or that a compliant media would assist them in keeping this terrible news from Neil's mum.

That week passed, other albums landed on my desk for review, and the Pet Shop Boys became rich and famous. But still the story wasn't entirely over. Repeated requests for an interview were deflected with sundry excuses. I was beginning to acquire the reputation of the man who lost *Time Out* the Pet Shop Boys interview. I met Tennant at a party and he promised that the Pet Shop Boys would give an interview to *Time Out* to coincide with their much-vaunted live tour, although this had been cancelled so many times that the promise was little more than obfuscation.

I guessed that there was something more fundamental at issue when another gay journalist, the late Kris Kirk, explained that he had had to sign an agreement not to discuss their private lives in return for an interview with the Pet Shop Boys. Either Neil still hadn't come out to his mum, or something else was at stake here.

Seven years on, it would appear that Tennant still hasn't had that heart-to-heart with his mother. (He did, of course, quote – come out – unquote to *Attitude* magazine in August 1994, but in such an eerily detached and reluctant manner that I believe these arguments still stand.) The Pet Shop Boys have yet to make any public statement about their sexual orientation, although they have managed to position themselves in such a way that their sympathies are unambiguous – collaborations with Derek Jarman, appearances at Clause 28 fundraisers, discussing the significance of disco on a gay television arts show – but they still do not intend actually to commit themselves verbally in a way that might set the hounds of Fleet Street on their trail. The act is akin to someone sidling around the back of a school class photograph, escaping one position to appear in another.

Given the content of their albums, and the moral climate of the times (however conservative), this is an extraordinary state of affairs. Ten or more years ago, their caution might be understandable (although, although; Tom Robinson had done major spade work in the mid-1970s). In the early 1990s, however, we look back on a good fifteen years when homosexuality was regarded as a commonplace among rock and pop performers. It is true that lesbian performers have been notable by their absence – only three come instantly to mind: Mathilde Santing, Phranc and k.d. lang – but an entirely different set of social and economic pressures comes into play when one contemplates the experience of lesbian performers. Yet so much of the last two decades of popular music has involved the participation of gay men that it would be impossible to complete the list. Bronski Beat, Frankie Goes to Hollywood, Culture Club, Blancmange, Soft Cell, Erasure are only the cream of first-division bands wholly or significantly composed of queers.

And yet, in word if not in deed, the Pet Shop Boys still feel a need to obscure or elide certain facts, and to deflect questioning on the matter. We are a little too far down the road for the commonplace rhetorical assertions normally associated with such situations: it's nobody's business but my own; it's my private life; why does it matter?; I don't have to tell you/explain/justify myself. It is almost as if Tennant and Lowe have decided that doing something isn't so bad as long as you don't actually name it (a concept familiar to anyone who has spent any amount of time in or around the closet).

However, if they are reluctant to name it, their career has been studded with references, some sly, many others overt, to queer culture. It is difficult (and perhaps actually impossible) to contemplate a pre-homosexual Pet Shop Boys. From 'Later Tonight' off *Please* to 'One in a Million' off *Very*, these are songs sung by men to other men. Heterosexual songwriters just don't write songs that way, employ such language, entertain such contingencies, structure relationships in certain ways, negotiate culture (big or small c), mediate experience, in short conduct the manoeuvres of bricolage, the act of cladding ourselves with social meaning, in that fashion. The Pet Shop Boys are careful to leave genders vague, a precaution that will enable them, when cornered, to say that a reference to a 'boy' not being the right person for the subject of a song could be addressed to a woman as much as to a man. (I would argue, however, that you don't meet that many women at that sort of night in Heaven.) This may in part be our old friend the sliding signifier – when the meaning of something you say has changed by the time I hear it – but again this would be incredibly naive of them. Indeed, given their cleverness and perhaps overdeveloped sense of irony, it would seem the height of carelessness.

Interpretation becomes a hazardous sport when played in the vicinity of the Pet Shop Boys, not least because they play a constant game of hide and seek with fans, critics and any other observer looking for the 'meaning' of the Pet Shop Boys. Fierce anti-rockists, as we used to say in the dear old days of the new wave, they insist that theirs is honest-to-goodness pop. Thus an MTV 'rockumentary', as the satellite channel calls them, on the duo became, wittily, a 'popumentary'. While they dismiss any claims to weighty intellectual meaning, they very much want their music to be taken seriously as quality entertainment. The anti-intellectual pose, anyway, is itself part of an elaborate act; anyone who plants coy, throwaway references to Edmund Wilson's study of the Russian revolution, *To the Finland Station*, in a hit single ('From Lake Geneva ...'), isn't playing the game with all their cards on the table.

From their inception, the Pet Shop Boys proceeded along lines developed from what Tennant observed as a journalist on *Smash Hits*. Because they are pure pop, Pet Shop Boys albums do not come with lyrics on the sleeve. Lyrics (or, heaven help us, lyric sheets!) equal meaning-of-life songs equal rockist brain death. Lyrics might encourage unhealthy thinking among fans who, in any case, are far too busy having a good time to sit down and contemplate a Pet Shop Boys lyric.

Similarly, the packaging of Pet Shop Boys, both the performers and their product, is carefully constructed. Cryptic (in fact meaningless) but arty in a *Vogue* photoplate kind of way, it appeals to the sense of decorativeness without actually bothering us with any content, or narrative. It invites us to decode then denies that there was anything there to decode in the first place. Pet Shop Boy iconography is King's Road shops, West End nightclubs, hazily filmic, sexually ambiguous. The montage for *Please* is one long semiotic tease on the subject of glamour and sexuality (although *Very* is a Van der Graaf Generator gatefold). Pet Shop Boy iconography quotes, or rather alludes, but so obliquely that you'd be impertinent to suggest as much. Just as with their music, which sometimes seems to be noise talking *about* music (be it the Isaac Hayes guitars or the furtive attempts to sound like the Beatles' 'All You Need Is Love' on *Behaviour*), they play a game of pretending/not-pretending so subtle that you almost suspect that, far from being a nightclubbing gadfly, Tennant might in fact spend much of his spare time swotting up on Jean Baudrillard.

Having sidled round the back of the school photograph, the Pet Shop Boys now occupy a curious space where they probably feel comfortable to have the queerness of their work discussed – the films with Derek Jarman, the battles with overseas censors, the sublime gender-switch subversion of U2's 'Street with No Name' – without having it named. It's old hat, a non-topic, stale news. It is almost as though the Pet Shop Boys are, as it were, post-out. The debate about their ambiguous sexuality is already over, without actually having taken place. They even crack jokes about it. In *Literally*, Chris Heath's book about life on the road with the Pet Shop Boys, they refer to a backstage interview in Hong Kong (for *Time Out*, as it happens, by a heterosexual stringer who wasn't about to rock the boat by asking controversial questions) as 'one of those "don't ask them about their sex life" interviews'. The controversy about their 'sex lives' has already happened, at some point in the past, where it has imploded into a black hole. 'We' no longer talk about it. It's almost the perfect arrangement, coming out's answer to surrogate parenting. Yet Heath's book remains the most uninformative and perhaps even dishonest pop book ever written. On the road with the Pets is just like on the road with a thousand other pop groups. Except other groups have private lives, husbands, wives, girl or boyfriends. Not the Pets. I call it the 'room of my own'/'day in the life' syndrome. When these generic magazine features cover heterosexuals, and the odd out queer, the room of their own or the day in their life features other people, who gave them the things in that room of their own, and who do things like dinner or work with them in that day in their life. Closets stick out a mile in these features: the contents of their room have materialized there anonymously, or perhaps have been planted on them. There are no intimate relationships encountered during that day in their life, only an echoing absence. In fact, they might as well have a neon sign flashing on and off that says 'Spot the missing boyfriend/girlfriend!'

Thus it is in life on the road with Chris Heath and the Pets. An intimate moment with the Pets is a ride in a limo, or perhaps a shopping trip. Straight friends will eagerly help them maintain the pretence (one such scolded my Stalinistic attitudes towards the Pets by saying, 'But they give a lot of money to AIDS charities, you know!' as though this either exonerated them politically or made me an utter beast for daring to comment) and gay friends, themselves perhaps not too certain of how they stood on the outing issue, would not presume to speak up.

The Pet Shop Boys are, in fact, a prime example of the open secret/glass closet theory of American writer Eve Kosofsky Sedgwick. In her book *Epistemology of the Closet*, Kosofsky Sedgwick points out that not even the smuggest politico is totally out. There are always people – work or school colleagues, distant relatives, neighbours, acquaintances, officials, people we have yet to get to know and so on – with whom we feel neither the need nor the desire to share our sexual orientation.

Exploring the cultural construction of the closet – an enclosure designed for containment as much as a bunker to keep things out, she says, and built by heterosexual society as much as by the beleaguered homosexual – Kosofsky Sedgwick pursues the idea of the open secret, the well-known little-known fact, the site where we argued the outing debate until things became a little too hot and we retreated behind a wall of well-meaning platitudes. The open secret – a well-known figure's homosexuality, for example – precludes any open discussion of the matter, or at least it does here in Britain while people cleave to the half-baked liberal mantra that no one has the right to drag someone else out of the closet. This is of course the compassionate line to take when someone really is in the closet and feeling that they have good reason to be there. When the closet walls become opaque, because the individual is only in there because of convenience, career or cowardice, and when in fact the closet becomes more a roomy *pied-à-terre*, used for weekends and the occasional overnight stay, then it is no longer a true closet but one made of glass. The ghastly English malaise of good manners effectively seals the closet shut, and it can sometimes take explosive charges – usually ignited on the steps of magistrates' courts by grinning journalists – to open it.

If the glass closet is kept sealed, it can soon be transformed from an open secret into what Kosofsky Sedgwick calls the empty secret, a secret that has lost the power to shame, embarrass or damage. A good example of an empty secret would be the homosexuality of Kenneth Williams, something guessed or presumed, but never spoken of. There are few true empty secrets involving homosexuals in pop. Boy George and Freddie Mercury might have been contenders, until their status became problematic, the one because of a heroin habit, the other a carefully hidden AIDS diagnosis. By keeping schtumm for the best part of a decade, refusing even to entertain discussion of their sexual orientation, the Pet Shop Boys are virtually home and dry with their empty secret intact. And yet . . .

I may seem to have mainly harsh things to say about the Pet Shop Boys personally. My opinion of them as people is that of George Orwell's famous essay on Salvador Dali; love the art, loathe the artist (although I am fully aware that I fail to fulfil my role in the simile: I am no Orwell to their Dali). Yet it is too complicated a story to be left to mere political difference. For a start, they have produced so much fine pop music, and pop music which has stood out from the mainstream, even if it has at times been baldly postmodern, playing the ironic quotation game with style but little passion or engagement. The video of 'Street with No Name' is, I believe, a landmark in queer art, undermining the impassioned laddishness of U2's original song, first with the segue into Andy Williams's 'Can't Take My Eyes Off of You', then with the genderfuck imagery of Tennant's heavily made-up face disappearing in and out of a dissolve. (To do them justice, U2, a favourite target of Tennant's campaign against earnest rock'n'rollers, are not altogether ignorant of queer culture. During the time they spent in Berlin recording *Achtung Baby*, they were sufficiently impressed by Berlin's gay scene to dress up in drag and as Sisters of Perpetual Indulgence for that album's artwork.)

Above all, however, the Pets' lyrics, never committed to paper for perusal, left to disappear with each passing bar, add up to a canon which, when considered as a whole (something they probably wouldn't welcome), might unintentionally outline a *langue d'amour* for the modern homosexual. Where a songwriter like Jimmy Somerville trades in camply renovated heterosexual soul cliché and a lyric form that has developed from the moon-June school, Pet Shop Boy lyrics, from 'Later Tonight' to 'One in a Million', when considered as the work of a homosexual, speak to, if not a modern gay sensibility, then a modern gay experience, albeit young, middle-class, urban and white. The acute sense of longing, the droll and sometimes acerbic view of relationships, and the social observation, while sometimes hamstrung by doggerel, are, I believe, unmistakably queer. It is unlikely that a heterosexual listener would glean this information, nor are the Pet Shop Boys about to draw their attention to it.

When asked about influences and traditions, they have often invoked the figure of peekaboo queer Noel Coward, who got away with murder in his work while maintaining a vigorously straitlaced public visage. (Coward may have written *Private Lives*, but he was also the director of *In Which We Serve*.) The Pet Shop Boys may fall short of Coward's wit and sophistication, but they very much fit the bourgeois English tradition of discreet perversion and collusion with the establishment. The Pet Shop Boys may give a lot of money to AIDS charities, but they also feel an overwhelming need to keep quiet about it. This may be modesty, for they distrust the ostentatious compassion of Live Aid and other such charity events. But this modesty, if modesty it really is, has become hostage to their refusal to make a simple statement about their sexuality.

In 1994, I would have thought that enough had happened to make such dissembling unnecessary. Perhaps the Pet Shop Boys represent a new conservativism, post-Clause-28, post-Thatcher, in the era of AIDS. Yet there is enough, perhaps even overwhelming, evidence that this need not be the case. In particular, the triumphal success of Erasure, with the unabashedly out Andy Bell, suggests that, whatever the misgivings of earlier gay musicians, popular success can be achieved without compromising one's sexuality or one's honesty.

The Erasures of this world, however, seem to be the exception rather than the rule. Yet from this desk, Erasure seem to offer irrefutable evidence that queer musicians need not hide themselves or resort to code. Others have done so and, as I hope we will see in this book, survived.

Chapter two

Burying Benjamin Britten

'We are, after all, queer & left & conshies, which is enough to put us, or make us yet put ourselves, outside the pale.'

● *Peter Pears, in a letter to Benjamin Britten, July 1963, quoted by biographer Humphrey Carpenter.*

I MUST confess to serious misgivings in approaching the subject of Benjamin Britten. It seemed that no survey of queer contributions to twentieth-century music could really disregard him, although the task of including Britten is made problematic by a number of factors. Historicity, or faithfulness to historical accuracy, presents an almost insurmountable barrier. How can the modern queer imagine what it would have been like to have lived as a homosexual in the 1930s, 1940s or 1950s? Edmund White has written that the modern homosexual is an invention of the postwar American and European sensibility, utterly different from his earlier incarnations. In the 1990s, it is apparent that the 1950s homosexual is distinctly different from his 1960s counterpart, and that cultural and ideological differences exist between homosexuals who established their cultural identity in the 1970s, 1980s and 1990s. Benjamin Britten and I might just as well have lived on different planets.

11: Burying Benjamin Britten

In a sense, we did. Coming from a lower working-class background, for years I associated classical music with middle-class privilege and power. Class, sexuality and the classical music world make a controversial combination, not least because consensus attitudes in this milieu tend to reflect some of the most conservative opinions of the time. While classical music has its liberal evangelists and proselytizers, consuming classical music is itself a hobby predicated on a system of ruthless snobbery, an infinitely gradated hierarchy of superiorities – conception, execution, interpretation, even the listener's ability to appreciate a work – given over to, no, supine at the feet of, nineteenth-century Romantic aesthetics, with rules set by the upper classes in the same century, an art or act of culture often distinguished solely by its social and intellectual exclusivity, and – quite literally – by its power to exclude. It relies on finely gradated hierarchies of education, social position and power, and peer group 'taste', which is why it attracts so many social climbers and train spotters. If I go to classical concerts these days, when I listen to the voices in the bar I hear the grinding machinery of the British class system at work. Even in the gents' at a Philip Glass opera, those Kensington and Chiselhurst accents have me dreaming of grenades.

Britten and Pears, then, might appear beyond the pale to someone of the same age and background as the surviving Sex Pistols, and indeed I came originally to bury Benjamin Britten, not praise him. Yet there is something about the nature of Britten and Pears, as suggested by that opening quote from the letter, about the public perception and construction of their homosexuality, which intrigues. Researching their careers and life together, I found myself being won round, if only partially, by the dead Britten and his lover Pears. I doubt, however, that either man would have welcomed the attention.

The reality of their contemporary public profile is difficult and perhaps impossible to define; even the first-hand reports of family, friends and colleagues are mediated by their desire to edit the Britten/Pears story so that it appears in the best (or, in some vengeful instances, the worst) possible light. Seemingly benign facts can become landmines; what we might surmise or decode as meaning x in the 1990s may not have been surmised or decoded at all fifty or sixty years ago. Events retain their integrity but what happens between the event and our interpretation of the event is a postmodern theme park with the latest white-knuckle rides.

The term 'public' should be promptly qualified, because Britten and Pears did not live openly as a gay couple, although considering the laws and social strictures of the years in which they lived together they were as quietly assertive of themselves as anyone could be given the circumstances. I am aware that their homosexuality may not have been the sort of homosexuality as figured among gay men today, and that homosexuality had a wholly different meaning then than it does now. However, looking at the traditional models of homosexuality available at the time, their relationship does not involve the age difference of the classical pederastic relationship, nor is there the class difference said to typify an earlier configuration of homosexuality. To all intents and purposes, Britten and Pears appear to have embarked on a one-to-one relationship akin to many gay relationships today. Daringly, they even shared a double bed in their bedroom at Aldeburgh, and made no secret of this among their friends.

Kosofsky Sedgwick's theory of the open secret/glass closet might also apply to Britten and Pears, although in drastically altered circumstances. Homosexual sex between two consulting males over twenty-one in private (defined around the time of the 1967 Sexual Offences Act as a locked property, i.e. an entire building, in which the two were alone) was legalized only in the last decade of Britten's life. It is difficult for anyone who did not live through those times to imagine the experience of homosexuals born in the early part of the century. While gay culture existed in private clubs, public toilets and cruising grounds, and gay men did of course meet, fall in love and live together, all these activities were fraught with the danger of blackmail, assault, arrest, imprisonment (sodomy carried the possibility of a life sentence, gross indecency two years) and social ruin. It is a measure of no mean fortitude that gay men managed to live at all under such conditions, and I believe we can detect a certain moral courage, however much Britten and Pears may have been part of the middle-class artistic establishment, in their taking the risk of conducting their relationship this way.

Although they did not give a name to it, Britten and Pears's sexuality was public enough for a stranger to scrawl an abusive 'pansy!' on a poster for a recital they gave in London early in the 1940s. Indeed, Britten's most recent, and most accomplished, biographer, Humphrey Carpenter, writes that their first ever performance together was taken by some as an announcement of their personal involvement. They met at the Royal College of Music in London, when Britten was twenty and Pears twenty-three. Britten was already involved in an unhappy relationship with the composer Lennox Berkeley. Britten stumbled into Pears's social circle, just as he had into that of Auden and Isherwood, and the friendship developed into what Britten would later refer to as a marriage. (While other biographies of Britten sometimes let things slip, I am indebted mainly to Humphrey Carpenter's candid life of the composer for most of this information.) Their sexuality must, eventually, have become apparent to family and friends after the two set up home together, first in London, then in their extended visit to America (where their hosts presumed them to be a gay couple) and again on their return, although it is unlikely that their relationship would have been described as anything more than friendship, collaboration or the myriad euphemisms people attached to homosexuals in their social circles. When Britten's mother died in 1937, he used the occasion of winding up her domestic affairs as an excuse to come out to his older brother Robert, and it appears to have been common knowledge that his sister Barbara was, for at least a part of her adult life, a lesbian.

It is possible that Britten was homosexual from an early age. His sister Beth, in her memoir of him, recalls that in their pre-teens they both had a crush on a Grenadier Guards bandleader who conducted a military band on the bandstand at Lowestoft on the Suffolk coast, where the Britten family home still stands on the seafront. It is impossible to measure what psychological weight we might place on a pre-teen crush, but for brother and sister to have discussed a shared infatuation does suggest a certain queer predilection in the sibling who was attracted to a member of his own sex. The singer Joan Cross believed that Britten had probably been born homosexual. Although he later told one acquaintance that he had been raped by a master at public school (one of two or so strange, apocryphal tales he told about his past; another was that his father had been a homosexual who made him cruise young boys for him. Neither tale was considered likely by those who ought to have known), his school career was largely uneventful. He began composing music at the age of nine, and in both junior and secondary schools developed strong attachments to other, younger, boys. These were – and, it would appear, remained throughout his life – platonic in the modern sense, although there is some hearsay evidence to suggest that, had his own reserve not got in the way, he might have consummated one or two of these relationships. It is possible that Britten was indeed a pedophile, who either did not act on his desires or managed to suppress them. With just one exception, all the young boys with whom Britten had these intense friendships attest that the composer was never more than fatherly or avuncular towards them, and that his affections never strayed into the realm of eroticism. Only one young friend, Jonathan Gathorne-Hardy, said that Britten had played an elaborate game of seduction with him. If Gathorne-Hardy had been willing, he tells Carpenter, 'We would have ended up in that double bed.'

It is unlikely that much would have happened in the double bed, for Britten was a boy lover who had a courtly ideal of the innocent youth, even though some of his operas involved placing innocent youth in positions of extreme, and in the case of *Peter Grimes* fatal, jeopardy. When Britten complained of the horrors he had to go through dealing with the studio system when composing music for the film *Love from a Stranger*, he said afterwards that he would never do another film score, unless he was asked to score a film of one of Arthur Ransome's Swallows and Amazons novels for children. The choice of Ransome – begetter of John and Susan, Titty and Roger, and the tomboyish Blackett sisters – perhaps gives an impression of the innocent child still in the adult Britten, although he was not without a dark side. On a number of occasions he unceremoniously dumped these young companions when they grew too mature, once arriving at the young friend's family home with a new munchkin pal in tow.

This was no different, however, to his treatment of adults. Few people who worked with or for Britten escaped his temper. Britten was a perfectionist, and musicians who did not live up to his requirements were also unceremoniously dumped, usually by management hatchet men and women doing Britten's dirty work for him. Once the Aldeburgh Festival became established in the 1950s, some complained that a nasty cliquish culture developed around Britten and Pears, with an ever-changing cast of favourites, flunkies and the fallen, the last of whom would be mercilessly blanked by the in crowd. One former collaborator, the writer Ronald Duncan, even went so far as to describe the atmosphere as 'reminiscent of Berchtesgarten', although this begs the question when was Ronald Duncan last a house guest of Adolf Hitler and Eva von Braun.

This ugly side of Britten – not so ugly, however, that the fallen could not find it in their hearts to forgive him, as most of them did – stemmed from his insecurities, about his talent, and what appears to have been a dualistic attitude to his sexuality. The conscience that had driven Britten to organize a protest against caning and write an essay criticizing bloodsports (marked zero) at school, and which led him into dalliances with the left in the 1930s and conscientious objection in the Second World War, probably buoyed his confidence in the essential decency of his relationship with Pears, and indeed his affection for his young friends. Yet there was also a conformist streak in Britten, and one which put their 'marriage' and his fondness for boys in an entirely different light. He startled at least one close friend by casually implying that his relationship with Pears didn't really mean anything; more, he hoped that Peter might one day get married. He even named a possible 'wife' for Pears, the singer Kathleen Ferrier. Like the apocryphal tales of school rape and cruising boys for his father, the contemporary reader can only put these statements down to a sudden, passing, crisis of nerves, self-doubt or old-fashioned guilt. A number of acquaintances have commented that whereas Pears seemed perfectly content in his sexual orientation, Britten was not entirely at ease as a homosexual. Some observers have read later works, such as *Death in Venice* and *The Burning Fiery Furnace*, as justifications of his innocent love of boys and, by extension, his homosexuality.

Consideration of this, too, is often confounded by the oddly public nature of the Britten–Pears marriage and Britten's affection for young boys. While much of the Britten material could be safely explained away as mere literature, some picked up on the darker themes in his work. One family acquaintance asked a collaborator if he couldn't persuade Britten to stop writing operas that involved young boys. The director Neil Mackerras commented to a friend on the number of young boys in the cast of *Noye's Fludde*. The comment got back to Britten, who confronted Mackerras, saying, 'Because I like to be with boys, and because I appreciate young people, am I therefore a lecher?' Discussing the same subject with a friend, Britten said, 'It's as if I was stealing money out of the till!' His indignation, and the public discussion of the topic, is a measure of the openness of Britten about his friendships, at least in close circles. Later in his life, Britten commented to Gathorne-Hardy, 'It's often a problem that these youngsters seem to think I want to go to bed with them.' A comment suggesting that Britten sited his affections elsewhere than the double bed.

This private candour points up a greater dualism in Britten's life; the desire to rebel and the need to conform. At school, he mustered enough self-confidence to protest against caning and write a polemic against bloodsports. His teenage diaries show that he also felt unequivocal affections towards other, younger boys, and he confided to his diary, in coded fashion, that these were homosexual feelings. On the surface, however, he was also a conventional, obedient and amiable young middle-class boy.

On leaving the Royal College of Music, he became a left-winger and pacifist after stumbling into the Auden–Isherwood set, and actively involved himself in artistic projects in the pacifist and left movements. There remains, however, the probability that Britten may have been out of his depth with the left in 1930s Britain. When, during the build-up to the Second World War, he and Pears went to America, where Pears had work engagements, the two appeared to be following Auden and did not seem to be really thinking through the consequences for either of them should war break out. When it did, they decided to stay in America, as friends urged them to. As a result, a great deal of bad publicity accreted to Britten's reputation. Yet Britten was committed enough to compound this, when he and Pears returned to Britain and declared themselves conscientious objectors, submitting to the hostile objector hearings, which interrogated pacifists about their ethical reasons for resisting combat work and tried to catch them out when questioning them about their reasons for refusing even non-combat work. Yet despite this seemingly anti-establishment behaviour, socially Britten was never happier than when hand in hand with the establishment. (He told Michael Tippett, with apparent dismay, that he could have been a Court composer 'but for my pacifism and homosexuality'.) It is perhaps a measure of his charmed life that this never really caused Britten more problems than those already mentioned.

As far as his homosexuality is concerned, Britten appears to have had no qualms about his desires, only about how others might perceive them. Here again, however, he seems to have been either happily unaware, or careless, about allowing queer themes to surface in his work from early in his career, dating from his settings of poems from Rimbaud's *Illuminations*, an interest sparked by Auden.

It was, of course, Britten's operas, notably *Billy Budd*, *The Turn of the Screw* and, notoriously, *Death in Venice* which addressed themselves to queer topics or pulsed with queer subtexts. Britten appears to have been content for these works to be received, as dutiful dullard British audiences and critics duly received them, simply as dramatic musical settings of classics in modern literature. In *Billy Budd*, the hapless sailor Billy is figured in homoerotically charged situations with both Captain Vere and the evil Claggart. In *The Turn of the Screw*, there are hints of unnamed perversions committed against the two young charges by the dead housekeeper and the manservant. And, of course, in *Death in Venice*, ailing composer Von Aschenbach spends a visit to the city haplessly pursuing a vision of beauty around the city – a boy, Tadzio, barely into his teens. The very literariness of these works provided an excuse should anyone raise any untoward questions about their tone, although the stoic British never did raise any untoward questions, in public at least. The theme of innocence abused runs like a thread through Britten's work, although in the above-mentioned operas the queer subtext could safely be ascribed to Herman Melville, Henry James or Thomas Mann. Britten was 'only' setting them to music. Yet the theme recurs in Britten's own works with less-famous texts, like *Peter Grimes*, *Albert Herring* and *Noye's Fludde*.

As far as the British press and chattering classes were concerned, this was all literature, culture, high art, and absolutely nothing to do with what Benjamin Britten might or might not like to get up to in the perilous privacy of his bedroom. If the themes ever were discussed by British critics, it was in terms of Byronic or classical terminology; code of sorts to those of a certain class and background, dead words to the multitude. It would take years, decades even, before domestic critics and observers would begin to discuss the issues at the core of Britten's work and life, and it would take until the 1990s before any biographer would honestly address Britten's sexuality and his relationship with Peter Pears. Yet outside prudish and infantile Britain these topics were being discussed as early as 1954. That year, reviewing the Venice production of *The Turn of the Screw*, the reviewer from the French newspaper *L'Express* wrote of 'the composer's customary intense preoccupation with homosexual love and the futility of struggling against it'. Humphrey Carpenter believes that this is the first time that homosexuality was mentioned in print in connection with Britten. Outside the gay and alternative media, it might also be one of the last. Even when both Britten and Pears were dead their life and work together was handled with gloves or tongs, and never given a name that was anything more than a coy euphemism. As is common in these circumstances, those who held the information thought that naming it was akin to smearing the reputations of the dead.

Enough smearing went on in private, anyway. William Walton spoke bitterly about Britten being offered a job at the Royal Opera House in Covent Garden, saying that there were already enough buggers in the place, and he apparently believed that there was a homosexual mafia at work in the music world, led by Britten and Pears. (Friends say that Britten never favoured people because of their sexuality or attractiveness; his ruthless hiring and firing practices would seem to bear this out.) Walton and his cronies, among them Constant Lambert, who would father queer pop entrepreneur Kit Lambert, invented homophobic jokes about the Britten–Pears duo, renaming Britten's work as *Bugger's Opera*, *Twilight of the Sods* and *Stern of the Crew*, which at least appeals on the level of a spoonerism. Walton, doomed to be remembered as the lightweight responsible for *Façade*, can have been motivated only by bitterness and envy.

Figures orbiting at the edge of the Britten solar system held that *Death in Venice*, in particular, was a coded paean to pedophile desire, intended to titillate fellow covert pedophiles. Yet a figure like Donald Mitchell, who, along with the other members of the fallen, would have good reason to speak ill of Britten, comes to his defence, writing of the work, 'I have often wondered ... whether ... he was not just referring to the opera's frank avowal of his own Tadzio-oriented homosexuality but also to the obligatory consequential constraints, the absence of which ... was ultimately Aschenbach's undoing.' This, says Carpenter, suggests that *Death in Venice* was more an anguished autobiographical tract by Britten, an account of the tension and guilt Britten felt because of his feelings for boys, and an oblique justification of his (honourable) intentions. The presence of innocence in his work, then, might be as a light driving out the darkness around him. And as Carpenter points out, Aschenbach is the seduced, not the seducer. If the piece has to have a victim, it is Aschenbach, not Tadzio.

Britten was always uncomfortable about the discussion of sexuality, particularly homosexuality, and even towards the end of his life still could not bring himself to mention his sexuality among his friends, even despite the change in public attitudes. He did, however, tell future biographer Donald Mitchell 'I want you to tell the truth about Peter and me.' The conformist Britten obviously wasn't above one last act of rebellion, although he no doubt imagined this one would be posthumous.

Towards the end of his life, Britten told Pears that he was glad to see increasing public tolerance of homosexuality, and indeed the Aldeburgh Foundation is committed to encouraging improved attitudes towards homosexuals. But Carpenter reports Pears saying 'the word gay was not in his vocabulary ... he resented that [word], I think'.

When Britten died in 1976, the Queen sent a telegram of condolence to Pears. 'It's a recognition of the way we lived,' he told a friend, implying that the missive represented a kind of blessing from the establishment. In fact, the telegram was a private note (she sends hundreds of them, as this former telegraphist's fingers will attest) from a member of a royal family with more than its fair share of queers among its acquaintances. The establishment was by no means willing to recognize the way Britten and Pears lived.

The *Guardian*, at least, was kind. The paper's classical music critic Edward Greenfield called Pears Britten's 'life-long friend', and in the same edition Michael Tippett wrote 'I loved him: but not with the selfless loyalty and devotion of Peter Pears, whom we all must thank for his unremitting care.' Those in the know, at least, might read between the lines that Britain's sole liberal newspaper was attempting to handle the taboo topic with dignity.

Not so the *Sunday Telegraph*, which, because Britten died overnight on a Friday, carried the obit. Critic Bayan Northcott named Pears as a collaborator of Britten's, but did not refer to their relationship, even in terms of a friendship or long-term working partnership. Northcott took time to remind readers of Britten's radical background, and the problems he encountered when he returned to Britain during the Second World War and declared himself a conscientious objector. While eliding any hint of queerness, less still queer dignity, from the lifetime of Benjamin Britten, Northcott made space for a final malicious semaphore to his friends in the Home Counties. Commenting piously on the problems that Britten encountered because of his political beliefs, the writer closed by pausing, portentously, to add that 'From the explicitness of his last opera, *Death in Venice*, it is difficult not to infer a still more private anguish.' The sentence closes with the sound of nails being hammered into a coffin.

The *Times* obituary mentioned Pears as a collaborator, briefly, but spent more space on the friendship between Britten and his teacher Frank Bridge. The almost page-length obituary carried no reference, hint or sly allusion to what was a cornerstone of Britten's private life. Yet someone with power over the content of the obituary page also decided to have a last laugh at the expense of Benjamin Britten. Parked by the bottom of what must be a three-thousand-word Britten obit is a thousand-word think-piece on 'The Christian dilemma over homosexuality'. I cannot believe that this coincidence of features occurred because of anything less than malicious fun, and am certain that the conjunction of think-piece and obit must have caused droll humour among *Times* journalists the afternoon they laid that page out.

And this in the week when the Sex Pistols swore on British prime-time television, and in a year when the long hot summer had seen gays rioting in Earls Court to protest against police harassment. It was 'only' the press, of course, but for the public these were the last widely broadcast images and opinions of the dead composer. Between them, the qualities buried the queer Benjamin Britten more effectively than I might ever have done.

Compare the cautious-yet-incautious Britten to his life-long friend Michael Tippett, ten years his elder but considered a contemporary because the two men's careers coincide chronologically. Tippett also appears to have been homosexual from an early age, and at the age of fourteen caused a sex scandal at his public school which resulted in his parents putting him in another school. Tippett had written to his parents, unwittingly revealing the level of queer behaviour at his school. His incensed parents descended on the school, causing the departure of the then headmaster, whose replacement barely persuaded them to keep Tippett at school. Tippett's housemaster then forced him to name names in front of the entire school, an act made more problematic by the fact that Tippett himself was romantically involved with another boy at the time. The situation became intolerable, and Tippett decided that the only option was to reveal all to his parents, trusting that in their shock they would remove him from the school. At the age of fourteen, Tippett calmly informed his parents that he had lost, or perhaps more accurately disposed of, his virginity with another boy. Nearly seventy years before OutRage! adopted the slogan, the teenage Tippett was saying, in effect, we're here, we're queer, get used to it.

Tippett was a highly unconventional boy from an unconventional background; his mother was a Labour supporter and Suffragette who once used her husband's charge account at a London department store to purchase handbells for confusing the police at Suffragette demonstrations. Tippett decided that he was an atheist at the age of eight, and at a later secondary school refused all commands to participate in rough sports or cadet training corps. He agreed to accompany the school choir until his religious beliefs (or lack of them) forced him to abandon that too. Disliking the regime at this school, Tippett refused to do any work in his last year, instead studying in secret and passing exams in 'six or seven subjects, including Italian' at the London Matriculation Board, just to prove to his bewildered headmaster that he could study and succeed if he really wanted to.

Despite the scandal at his first public school, and despite having 'like all others to play various tricks', the young Tippett seems to have blithely continued to conduct himself as a homosexual with little or no regard for the mores or laws of the day. As a student at the Royal College of Music in London, he fell in love with a fellow student he met on a bus to a cricket match, and started writing him love letters without, it seems, even really thinking about it. The autobiography is a place where the fabulist, mythifier and bricoleur can have a field day, yet Tippett's autobiography *Those Twentieth Century Blues* paints a picture of its author as a figure who, like Wilde before him and Crisp after him, could not help but be himself. Tippett set up home with a gay partner while still a student at the Royal College of Music, and would argue the church's attitude to homosexuality with religious-minded friends. Michael Tippett was, in a word, *out*. 'In my youth,' he writes, 'my homosexual side revealed itself. I accepted it without reservation, as something instinctive and therefore natural.'

Like Britten, Tippett also became involved in left-wing politics, although at a more grass-roots level. He participated in work camp holidays for the urban poor, produced music for left-wing and pacifist events, and became involved with the Workers' Music Association, an organization which provided musical training and rehearsal space for those without the wherewithal to avail themselves of the conventional, costly, forms of musical training. He also joined the British Communist Party, and immersed himself in the literature of communism, although he left the party after Stalin's purges.

The first major love of Tippett's life was Wilf Franks, a painter and craftsman who had studied at the Bauhaus and travelled widely in Europe. Wilf was bisexual, and when he announced his plans to marry a young woman Tippett ended their relationship. From the way Tippett describes their relationship, Wilf was reluctant to give a name to their 'queer' – Tippett's term –

love, while Tippett was happily candid about his feelings. For the past thirty or so years, his partner – I am disinclined to intrude with any more precise adjective – has been the writer and critic Meirion 'Bill' Bowen. Tippett describes Meirion Bowen as a number of things – assistant, partner, manager, tour organizer, bodyguard, cocktail mixer – but avoids any stronger word to define their partnership. The tone of Tippett's letters to Bowen, some of which are published in his autobiography, makes clear his affection for Bowen, but when it comes to naming it Tippett seems to be suffering from GCS, the Glass-Closet Syndrome, which caused one famous actor to pen four volumes of autobiography in which he referred to his lifelong lover either as his 'secretary' or with a peremptory reference to the man's surname throughout. (GCS struck again in a recent biography of queer composer Samuel Barber, in which his lifelong lover, Gian Carlo Menotti, pops up throughout the book without a word to explain what he's doing there.)

The most interesting comparison between Britten and another twentieth-century gay composer, and there are plenty to choose from – Henze, Maxwell Davies, Goehr are just the tip of the iceberg – would be the American composer Ned Rorem, only ten years Britten's junior but for his time a one-man Queer Nation riot. Rorem's work is difficult to find in Britain today, although at the peak of his career his work was put on a par with the likes of Aaron Copland. He writes primarily in song form, setting pieces from Whitman, Roethke, Gerard Manley Hopkins and Paul Goodman, but also produced operas and adventurous orchestral works, such as *Eagles* and *Water Music*. He is still composing: he contributed a piece to the *AIDS Quilt Songbook* and recorded a new concerto in 1994.

Also precociously talented, Rorem was born with the good looks of one of Cocteau's gilded youths, and, one imagines, a temperament to match. Rorem studied with Poulenc in Paris in the 1950s, and also under Virgil Thomson, Darius Milhaud, Arthur Honneger and Copland. His diary of these years, *The Paris Diary*, published in 1967, scandalized musical and intellectual circles on both sides of the Atlantic with its casual, indeed flamboyant, indiscretions about the private lives of Rorem and his friends in the French capital.

He followed that a year later with his *New York Diary*, which recorded, among other things, several affairs, being beaten up by someone else's trick whom he picked up at a party, going down on Billie Holiday in a nightclub, a gleefully viscous account of a visit to one of New York's scuzzier bathhouses, and an incandescent love letter, some thirty pages long, to a French dentist who had recently dumped him, written in the manner that Rimbaud wrote to Verlaine and closing in a firework display of expletives ignited in the face of the lover who had spurned him. At times, Rorem's writing is mannered and florid, but at others his ruminations on queer love resemble the unwritten book buried beneath the anonymous narratives of Roland Barthes's *A Lover's Discourse*. While the closeted Barthes never dared name or give a gender to the obscure object of his desires – except in the fragments published posthumously as *Incidents* – Rorem cheerfully names and sexes his former lover, giving his profession and all-but publishing his address and phone number.

Even though Rorem was one of the *jeunesse d'orée*, if now an alumnus, and moved in fairly rarefied circles, the publication of these diaries was at odds with the spirit of the time, when the American gay rights movement was represented by the sober Mattachine Society and Daughters of Bilitis, and when the Stonewall riots were still a few years off. Queer literature was nothing new in the early 1960s, of course, but the courage, or plain recklessness, of Rorem's personal disclosures was remarkable. Again, however, these should be put into context, not least because Rorem was publishing during what was probably the greatest period of liberalism this century, and wasn't famous enough to draw fire from the far right.

There was also, it seems, a distinct difference between the public Rorem and the writer Rorem at his desk. During a BBC radio interview in 1978, Rorem rounded on the interviewer, who had been trying to coax him into discussing his sexuality. Asking about *The Paris Diary*, the interviewer wondered if his life in Paris had been gay in all senses of the word. 'Gay is your word, not mine,' Rorem snapped. 'I love the real meaning of the word,' he continued, calming to add the curious comment, 'I have had a gay life in every sense of the term, [but] it's difficult to say what I have already written about in words.' This may, however, have been Rorem wanting to keep the conversation on the topic of his music, which, as the interviewer announced rather tactlessly prior to the interview, wasn't very well known in Britain. It may also be, as Rorem commented himself in the interview, that his prose had become more careful while the 'hysteria' (his term) was now in the music. It should also be said that there is a distinct difference between the voice of Rorem in interview and that of the Rorem who wrote his diaries.

These misgivings aside, however, one can only marvel at Rorem's insouciant candour, even though he may have considered it less a political act and more a literary conceit. The gulf between his attitude and experience and those of Benjamin Britten cannot be explained by the mere ten years' age difference, although it probably could be explained by a few thousand miles of seawater and the different cultures they separate. Yet not even a body of water such as the Atlantic is necessarily a sufficient barrier to stop the spread of something as deadly as GCS.

Chapter three

A Minute's Noise for John Cage*

AS Peter Pears found out, obituaries are places where queers are buried in unmarked graves and where their lovers can expect to be Disappeared. Thus it was in the days following 12 August 1992, when it was announced that composer John Cage had died at the age of eighty. While the conservative press might be expected to look askance at the artistic reputation of a maverick like Cage, all the so-called quality papers devoted ample space to mourning his death. The *Daily Telegraph* pulled in its claws for an anodyne report on his life and achievements. The *Guardian* put the news of his death on the front page, and ran lengthy appreciations, one of which said Cage had 'the fertility of invention which marks the genius'. The *Guardian* also noted his collaboration of some forty years with the dancer and choreographer Merce Cunningham, adding that Cage lived in a New York loft apartment 'shared with Cunningham'. *The Times* published a fulsome obituary and even ran a leader article, 'Pray Silence for John Cage', which was actually very positive about Cage's contribution to music and to the ways we think about music.

What none of the papers said, however, was that John Cage was a queer, and that for the better part of the twentieth century he and Cunningham had been lovers. This is not, however, just

---

* With apologies to Kipper Williams, whose joke this is.

another example of subtle homophobic censorship: Cage himself colluded in the silence, and in a manner that is quite startling given the radicalism he pursued in so many other areas of his life.

Cage will no doubt be remembered in popular terms as the mischief-maker who 'composed' a totally silent piece of music, the much-misunderstood *4' 33"*, and innumerable other pieces in which outlandish objects were employed to produce bizarre and for some unpleasant noises. This, at least, was the reputation that dogged him through some fifty years in the media. The truth is rather different. While many of Cage's works did shock and amuse – the two reactions are anything but self-exclusive in Cage's philosophy – they also had a deadly serious intent and, for those who were prepared to listen, were often quietly revelatory about the nature of music and how we perceive it. Much of Cage's work involved systems of randomness and indeterminacy, music played or scored depending on the fall of the *I Ching*, or music generated by computers selecting passages at random; but much of it, such as the *Freeman Etudes*, and *Etudes Australes*, is also highly complex music requiring virtuosic performance.

Cage's influence spreads far and wide. His work for prepared piano in the 1940s looks forward to the work of Brian Eno and others in the 1970s and 1980s, and his earlier *First Construction (in Metal)* predates the metal-bashing bands of the 1980s, such as Test Dept and Einstürzende Neubauten, by a good half century. His experiments with electronic music, like those of Karlheinz Stockhausen, provide a backdrop for untold experimental rock groups, and for decades Cage presided over an American avant-garde that was to produce LaMonte Young, Terry Riley, Steve Reich, Philip Glass and Laurie Anderson. Directly and indirectly, his ideas about music continue to filter through the world of music, both serious and popular, and into other related arts.

Born the year before Benjamin Britten, in 1912, Cage began his musical career inauspiciously, as the twelve-year-old presenter of a Boy Scouts' radio show on Radio KNX in Los Angeles, on which Scout Cage would introduce other Scouts doing their musical party pieces. The Scouts had let Cage develop the show on his own. When it began to look successful, Scout HQ took over the running of the show, and it folded soon afterwards.

Cage's early efforts at music-making produced mainly dismay, to him and those about him. As he later confessed, he couldn't hold a tune and did not have an ear for melody or harmony. However, something in him made Cage persist, and with a happy-go-lucky confidence that seems to have guided him throughout his life, he learnt, or decided, to turn his disadvantages to his advantage. He attempted to pursue a vocation as a writer, but gave up and in frustration with the American education system persuaded his parents to pay for a trip to Europe.

In Paris, a chance encounter with a former teacher won Cage a contact at an architect's office, where he got a job working as an assistant. He dabbled in painting, and through a contact he was accepted as a piano student at the Conservatoire. He soon abandoned these studies, but was already immersing himself in all manner of music, from Bach to Stravinsky. When he returned to America in 1931, after eighteen months' travelling in Europe, Cage began writing his own music.

The composer who excited Cage most at the time was Schoenberg, who arrived in America in 1934, fleeing the spread of Nazism in Europe. The ever-impecunious Cage, who had to fend for himself when his inventor-father fell on hard times, managed to find himself a job as assistant to his teacher, the American composer Henry Cowell, in New York. Taking a look at Cage's compositions, Cowell told him the only teacher for him was Schoenberg. Cage petitioned Schoenberg, who finally relented, agreeing to teach him for free if he agreed to devote his life to music. There is some disagreement about Cage's actual relationship with Schoenberg. Some of his detractors denied that Cage ever studied with Schoenberg, but fellow students attest to his presence on a number of Schoenberg's courses. Cage grew to admire Schoenberg 'as a god'. He also grew to notice that gods sometimes have feet of clay, and soon found himself becoming estranged from Schoenberg's ideas. Cage struck out on his own, discarding Schoenberg's twelve-tone influence and making something all his own. This music, chiefly for percussion ensemble, was more akin to other music in the air at the time, such as the Futurist music of Marinetti and Russolo, and the groundbreaking work of Edgard Varèse (who would later exert a gravitational pull on, among others, Charlie Parker and Frank

Zappa). It is also possible that, under Henry Cowell, Cage had also discovered the gamelan music of Indonesia; certainly, some of his earliest prepared piano pieces sound like small gamelan ensembles.

At the time, in the mid-1930s, Cage was supporting himself with haphazard teaching work and odd jobs; at various times he was a gardener, a restaurant dishwasher and a cleaner at a YWCA. Then one day in early 1938, he was offered a job at a music school in Seattle. Here he met young dancer Mercier 'Merce' Cunningham.

By this time, Cage was already married. Three years earlier, in 1935, he had met a serious and beautiful young art student, Xenia Kashevaroff, when she visited a shop where Cage was working. He asked her out to dinner, and decided to use the dinner as an opportunity to ask her to marry him. She asked for time to consider, but shortly after accepted his offer and they were married in June 1935. Not much has been recorded about the marriage, but it would seem to have been a marriage of similar minds to the extent that Xenia became a member of Cage's ad hoc percussion ensemble.

Cage's official biographer, David Revill, reports that Cage's encounter with Cunningham in Seattle set in train a course of events which led to the collapse of his marriage five years later. Cage, Xenia and Cunningham worked together on a number of projects in Seattle, before Cunningham was called back to New York by work. Little is known – or has been said – about the intervening years, but by 1942 Cage's marriage was on the rocks, and Cage appears to have been teetering on the edge of a nervous breakdown. The marriage collapsed in 1944, and Cage and Xenia separated in 1945. At the suggestion of friends, Cage tried psychoanalysis, but found the initial encounter so alien that it put him off psychoanalysis for life. Coincidental to these events, Cage had also been enquiring into Eastern philosophy, and it is possible that the convergence of these forces put Cage on to the philosophical path that he would follow for the rest of his life.

Somewhere in all this, he and Merce Cunningham also managed to become lovers. It is difficult, if not impossible, to glean much more about their relationship since, as David Revill observes, 'the protagonists have kept the matter private'. He adds that, as recently as 1992, a young speaker at a conference at Stanford

University was censured by the chairman of the conference for mentioning Cage's homosexuality 'because' Cage does not mention it. As to the break-up with Xenia, Revill reports that 'a crisis of a marriage and of sexual orientation occurred' and stops there. Given that Cage had given Revill carte blanche to write his book, and given that Cage would read it before Revill passed it to his publishers, Cage must have come to a personal decision about this disclosure by proxy, while himself remaining silent.

Cage wasn't always so worried about his privacy – or, perhaps, the world wasn't so interested that he felt the need to keep schtumm. The only other reference to Cage's queerness in David Revill's biography is a brief but tantalizing reference to the Cage–Cunningham friendship with painters Robert Rauschenberg and Jasper Johns. In 1954, Rauschenberg and Johns became lovers, and Cage and Cunningham used to double-date with them, going out to bars in Greenwich Village. The quartet of Cage, Cunningham, Rauschenberg and Johns gang-handed and painting Greenwich Village red, or pink, must have been a sight to behold. Again, at the time no critic or journalist would have dared mention their homosexuality, yet this sole snippet from forty years of shared life suggests that Cage and Cunningham at some point actively enjoyed a homosexual lifestyle. There were certainly a number of prominent homosexuals among the Beats and New York school – Ginsberg and Frank O'Hara, for starters – for homosexuality to be accepted by the artistic community. Yet Cage decided to maintain a personal silence on the subject for the rest of his life.

There is an argument that John Cage did not 'have' to disclose his sexual orientation and specific partnership with another man. The argument proceeds to ask 'why' should he have to? Isn't it his own business? Shouldn't he have the right to remain private?

I would answer the above questions by asking, if Luciano Berio didn't feel a need to hide his marriage to singer Cathy Berberian, for whom he wrote a number of works, why should John Cage have felt the need to hide his relationship with Merce Cunningham, for whom he too wrote and dedicated a number of works? It doesn't improve a work to know that Berio and Berberian were married, but it tells us something about its creation, and the intention behind it, and perhaps increases our appreciation of it. Similarly, it does not radically alter a piece of music if we know that Cage and Cunningham were lovers, but it does tell us something about the composer's intent in writing the piece, and will help our appreciation of the work. Cage wrote numerous compositions for Cunningham, as well as non-musical literary pieces, such as the *62 Mesostics Re Merce Cunningham*, a mesostic being Cage's term (in fact a neologism invented by his friend Norman O. Brown) for word-patterns in a text. If an acrostic is a word made up of the first letters of a series of sentences, a mesostic, borrowing the Greek *meso* for middle, finds its patterns in the middle of words and sentences.

If someone is irrationally, pathologically obsessed with secrecy, I have to answer yes to all the above questions. Yet John Cage was none of these things, except when it came to his sexuality. Elsewhere in his life, Cage was outspoken on all manner of subjects: music, aesthetics, the creative process, world politics, eastern mysticism, ecology, macrobiotics, and the topic that made him the star of an Italian quiz show, mycology, or the cultivation, collection and consumption of mushrooms. Mushrooms were Cage's personal manna. In Italy in the 1960s, he went on a prime-time TV quiz for five weeks running answering questions on the subject, and became a media star as each week he got each question right, winning enough to buy himself a brand-new Steinway and a station wagon for Cunningham's dance company.

Cage cheerfully held forth about these topics on numerous occasions; in interviews, in his lectures – which, inevitably, came to be seen as extensions of his music, as music in their own right – and in his books: *Silence*, *M – Writings*, *X – Writings*, *A Year from Monday*, *Empty Words* and a collection of interviews, *For the Birds*. In these, Cage spoke or wrote at length about his career-long fascination with the works of James Joyce, Gertrude Stein and Henry David Thoreau, the first and last of whom presented texts that he would work with throughout his career. He discussed in detail his interest in Eastern philosophy, in particular the Zen teachings of Daisetz Teitaro Suzuki, whom he met in 1951/2 and who would have such a profound effect on his thinking. Cage also enthused regularly about his friend the *I Ching*, a portable oracle for every creative occasion (and an idea later borrowed by Brian Eno for his Oblique Strategies card set). Cage expatiated at length about the ideas of Buckminster Fuller and Marshall McLuhan, while declaring conventional politics useless. A libertarian anarchist in the Thoreau mould, he sometimes despaired of American democracy. He once refused to sign a petition against nuclear power, saying he wasn't interested in protesting against things that were wrong. He was interested in boycotting things out of existence, shampoo for example, and although he was interested in the Green movement he was suspicious of any group that vied for political power. For a good part of the 1970s, he was an outspoken Maoist, until Maoism fell from favour. When he fell ill with a career-threatening arthritis in the early 1970s, his friend and neighbour Yoko Ono advised him to visit a macrobiotic specialist. With the aid of cookery books given him by John Lennon, Cage beat the illness with macrobiotics, and became a lifelong convert to the system of not mixing yin and yang foods. A few times, his books even addressed the subject of sex, but in such a vague genderless way as to make them more metaphysical musings than anything addressing everyday human desire. And despite his disavowal of politics, as late as 1991 he could still write a mesostic about the war in former Yugoslavia quoting a friend who blames the Serb government for the conflict.

If these themselves weren't radical statements, then the Cage canon itself stands impeccable witness to the man's willingness to flout convention, flaunt perversion and court controversy. He invented the prepared piano – a piano with objects such as bolts or screws, pieces of metal or rubber inserted into the body to alter the sound made by hammer striking wire – by accident. In 1940, a dancer colleague needed a composer to provide music for a school performance. Cage was the only composer available, and there was space only for a piano on stage. Cage took an idea from his teacher Henry Cowell, who had begun investigating the noises one could make inside a piano, and customized a piano to give the dancers a rhythmic musical accompaniment.

In 1952, Cage and his colleagues at Black Mountain College invented the Happening, which would be taken up by the Fluxus Group. One day, they devised an event in the round during which Cage delivered one of his lectures from the top of a step-ladder, Cunningham danced around the audience, Rauschenberg hung a series of his white colour-field paintings from the rafters, David Tudor played piano, and films and movie stills were projected around the space.

The same year Cage premièred his notorious silent piece, *4' 33"*, in front of an audience in the upstate New York artists' colony of Woodstock. In fact, *4' 33"* is anything but silent, and was motivated by a visit Cage made to the physics department of Harvard University. Cage visited Harvard to investigate an anechoic chamber (David Bowie can be seen entering one on the sleeve of *Station to Station*), a sealed room whose surface is covered in sound-baffling materials which can absorb up to 99 per cent of ambient noise. Cage found that, far from being silent, the room proved very loud with two particular sounds, the deep bass pulse of his own blood system, and the high-pitched crackle of his own nervous system at work. So too the Woodstock audience found that *4' 33"*, a suite broken down into three parts, lasting 33 seconds, 2 minutes 40 seconds, and 1 minute 20 seconds, and drolly 'transcribed' for piano by David Tudor, was anything but silent. Its world première took place during a rainstorm, leaving the audience to contemplate wind, rain, and their own ambient noise. The New York performance was rather more demure, leaving the audience to listen to only their own coughs, rustles and whispers, and whatever ambient noises the building might contribute. Some urbane Manhattanites were outraged, others delighted. A German musician friend reports that, when he confessed to Cage backstage that the piece had stunned him into laughter, Cage beamed at him in delight.

Cage's work with random or aleatoric music, letting an external chance system dictate the procession of notes, bars or noises, is as radical an application to music as the cut-up/fold-in technique developed by Burroughs and Brion Gysin, which has been compared to scratch, hip-hop and sampling techniques. In some cases, it could be said to have a more direct and radical link to scratching and sampling than the cut-up. In a piece like *HPSCHD*, a computer file-name for Harpsichord and intended to be pronounced as Harpsichord, a computer deploys randomly selected segments of Mozart and others, and live musicians are enjoined by the score to contribute their own random and haphazard snippets of music. The result, originally accompanied by multi-screened projections of NASA space footage, is a dizzying three-hour swirl of dense noise, out of which pop delicate fragments of Mozart, only for the fragments to be sucked back into the seething row once more.

Above all, Cage proved that all noises are, in Brian Eno's phrase, 'possible musics'. Cage composed music for furniture, water and fire, buildings, constellations, toys, food processors, bird cages, plants, trains, a vast and boggling array of sound sources.

Stumbling across Cage's work for the first time, in the shape of an electronic realization of his *Fontana Mix*, was like discovering an encyclopedia describing a universe of sounds that I hadn't known existed until then. That was in my teens, and in the intervening years there have been few areas of music that I have explored – German avant-garde rock, electronics, minimalism, free music, *musique concrète*, ethnic forgery and the farther shores of punk – that didn't have John Cage's fingerprints all over them, or didn't carry an echo of Cage's elfin chuckle. Although a few years too young to really mourn either Hendrix or Lennon, I felt the loss of John Cage almost as badly as I did the loss of Miles Davis. The world became perceptibly darker, smaller, meaner, duller.

I only ever met Cage once, as a member of the audience during the London celebrations of his seventieth birthday. We sat a seat apart during a simultaneous performance of two or three of his pieces, during which musicians ran around a deconsecrated chapel in north London switching radios on and off at random, playing the outsides of grand pianos, and competing with assorted taped interventions around the room. The event was preceded by an announcement to the effect that Mr Cage did not allow any of his music to be tape recorded during performances. I laughed aloud at the notion of the avant-garde anarchist protecting his mechanical and performance copyrights, and Cage, noticing, grinned back. At the time, I did not even know John Cage was a homosexual. If I'd thought about it at all, I would have imagined Cage to be somebody's bearded and mischievous grandad. It took a colleague's careless gossip about Cage and Cunningham living together even to raise the topic.

It is possible that the asceticism of Cage's lifestyle precluded any discussion of his sexuality, just as it is possible that, like John Cheever, Cage felt himself too old to join in with the queer culture wrought by gay liberation. It may also be that Cage did not believe that politics, party or personal, had any part in art. He once said, with uncharacteristic acidity, of the English left-wing composer Cornelius Cardew, whose works, such as *The Great Learning*, mixed avant-garde techniques with proselytizing left-wing politics, that Cardew didn't do the revolution any good nor did he do music any good. 'Art,' he once told a student reporter, 'has continually had the function of awakening people to the life around them.' But not, it seems, to the composer's sexuality.

Cage appears to have been able to compartmentalize his homosexuality away from all the other aspects of his life and career. David Revill is baffled by Cage's reluctance, especially when compared with his friend and colleague Lou Harrison, who has been out for years. While on one level that is terribly sad, on another Cage does at least seem to have managed to achieve what he set out to do. Towards the end of a life which saw him mixing with the likes of Duchamp, Ernst, Mondrian, Breton, Moholy-Nagy, Mies van der Rohe, Virgil Thomson and Harry Partch, Cage was able to say of his life, 'I have nothing to complain about. I've enjoyed it, the whole thing.' I can't help wondering, however, how much richer that life would have been had Cage not felt the need to hide so fundamental a part of that enjoyment.

Chapter four

Mannish-Acting Women, Woman-Acting Men

THERE were just two things, Bessie Smith sang in 'Foolish Man Blues', that she just couldn't understand. 'That's a mannish-acting woman, and a skipping, twisting woman-acting man.' In fact, as many of her friends and even some of her fans would have known, the Empress of the Blues was being less than honest in this chorus to her song. Smith herself sometimes behaved like the women she claimed not to understand. And she was accompanied on piano by Porter Grainger, a man who may not have skipped or twisted in public but who was certainly a queer.

The chorus to 'Foolish Man Blues' is actually a red herring. The man of the title, framed in a generic blues complaint about the uselessness of men, is a man who had been pursuing a young woman for a year and then, when she let him kiss her, jeopardized the relationship by boasting about it around town. The refrain may have been a mischievous diversion, a hint at her own ambiguous sexuality, or an ironic tease for her audience, who most certainly knew what Smith was talking about. Her biographer Chris Albertson states categorically that 'most urban blacks – whether they indulged or not – accepted homosexuality as a fact of life'.

Born in Chattanooga, Tennessee, in 1894, at least according to a date of birth she gave on a marriage application form, Bessie

Smith began her singing career about the time that John Cage was hosting Boy Scout jokes and bird noises on Radio KNX in Los Angeles. Like much black history of the period, information that today might be freely available about an individual has been lost for ever, leaving only hearsay and apocryphal anecdote about Smith's early life. One popular story about the beginning of her career, that she was kidnapped and groomed by Gertrude 'Ma' Rainey, has been dismissed by Chris Albertson, her most authoritative biographer, who points out that the two women couldn't have more different singing techniques than can be heard in their recordings. (Indeed, such is the texture of Rainey's voice that she might sometimes be mistaken for a male singer.)

According to Albertson, Bessie Smith had lost both parents and two of six siblings by the age of nine. She took to busking in the streets of Chattanooga to supplement the remaining family's meagre income. Her eldest brother, Clarence, entered a travelling negro minstrel show, and managed to win his sister an audition for the show when she was in her mid-teens. It was here that Smith first encountered Ma Rainey. Contemporaries described Bessie Smith as a born natural, and a natural, moreover, who at first seemed unaware of her considerable talents.

By the time Prohibition came into force in 1920, Smith was already a seasoned cabaret performer, now based in Philadelphia. As Smith's reputation burgeoned in the cabarets and musical tent tours, winning her the nickname of Empress of the Blues (her elder Ma Rainey had already been dubbed its Mother), an embryonic 'race music' market was branching off from the nascent record business, specializing in music by black performers which new label owners like the legendary W. C. Handy realized could be sold to black people. In blues as in punk, the big labels moved in once they recognized a market waiting to be exploited, and Bessie Smith was signed to the 'race' division of Columbia Records (later CBS and, now, Sony). She made such an impression on Columbia's race music division head, reports Albertson, that he 'sent' his race music A&R man south to 'get' Smith. Her first release, a version of 'Down Hearted Blues', sold over 780,000 copies in its first six months of release in 1923.

By this time, Bessie Smith was a sensation, and her career

was only at the beginning of an upward curve. Throughout the 1920s, up until the Depression began to take its toll on the entertainment industry, Smith could not record enough new records to please her fans, nor could she play enough dates to satisfy all those who wanted to see the Empress of the Blues perform live. Smith made several small fortunes from her work, but disposed of them, via her husband, Jack Gee, her family, and friends. A formidable opponent, and handy with her fists, as she needed to be in a relationship with a man like Jack Gee, she was also generous to a fault. Even when her career began an inevitable downturn during the Depression, Smith was still supporting three close relatives and, intermittently, her then former husband, Gee.

She recorded 'Foolish Man Blues' in 1927, and for all its claims to bemusement at the behaviour of what would then have been described as 'faggots and bulldaggers', she had known perfectly well the world and ways of mannish women and woman-acting men for at least three years. As Chris Albertson reports, barely a year into their marriage, Jack Gee began hearing rumours about his wife's exploits when he wasn't around. The rumoured events took place when Jack was off spending her money, pursuing his own attempts at showbusiness management or conducting his own, heterosexual, extra-marital affairs. At first, Smith's extra-marital activities involved men friends on the road, but quite soon they also involved women friends on the road too. Her first notable lesbian relationship, according to her niece Ruby Walker, was with a member of her troupe, Lillian Simpson, in 1926. Lillian Simpson was the daughter of a friend, and Smith gave her a job in her troupe because of that friendship.

Her travelling company spent Christmas 1926 on the road in Tennessee. By now, Smith was wealthy enough to own her own railway carriage, some 80 feet long, which transported the cast and crew from town to town and, crucially, saved them the problems of dealing with both a segregated transport system and hotels that refused to accommodate blacks. Smith threw a Christmas party for the women in the company, and evidently seduced Lillian Simpson at this party, leading her off on her own while the rest got drunk on eggnog. Her niece Ruby and Lillian shared a room on the train, but Lillian didn't return to her room that night. Simpson appeared to adjust to her relationship with Smith very quickly, even suggesting to roommate Ruby that she should try lesbian sex with another woman in the entourage, Boula Woods, wife of the show's musical director, Bill Woods. Things even got to the state where a jealous Boula Woods, misconstruing a harmless gesture between Ruby and another woman in the cast, warned her not to mess around with any other women in the troupe.

On another occasion, when the troupe was on the road in St Louis, Smith entered the dressing room that Ruby shared with Lillian, and embraced and kissed Simpson. Lillian jerked away, embarrassed. Smith rounded on her, snapping 'I got twelve women on this show and I can have one every night if I want it. So don't feel so important, and don't you say another word to me while you're on this show or I'll send you home bag and baggage.'

As a consequence of this showdown, Simpson tried to commit suicide by gassing herself in a hotel room, but Smith saved her and paid for her hospital treatment. Smith also brought her home from the hospital. As Ruby told Chris Albertson, 'From that day on, she didn't care where or when Bessie kissed her – she got real bold.'

Albertson reports that the relationship between Bessie and Lillian kept the prodigious drinker Smith 'relatively sober'. When the relationship ended, Smith let Simpson leave without a word of recrimination, and took herself and a group of her predominantly teenage young women performers to a 'buffet flat', a raunchier version of the traditional rent party. Buffet flats are mentioned in various examples of Harlem Renaissance literature, although only in passing, as though the reference itself is self-explanatory, as it would have been to contemporary readers. We have her niece Ruby to thank for a particularly vivid piece of reportage on a little-known corner of black and queer heritage culture.

The troupe were in Detroit, home to a particularly notorious buffet flat owned by a good friend of Smith's. Buffet flats had originally grown up as a network of comfortable places to stay for black Pullman porters, whose work found them turning up in strange cities at odd hours looking for somewhere that a black person might stay. Thanks to black entrepreneurial skills, the buffet flats transmuted into private fun houses where most illegal practices and substances could be procured for a price. They were, Albertson reports, owned mainly by women, and were noted for their security and the absence of violence or robbery.

The buffet flat that Smith took her girls to in Detroit was one that she would later immortalize in her 'Soft Pedal Blues'. As in most buffet flats, which were also known as good-time flats, boot-leg liquor was in constant supply, gambling a common pastime, dope – Albertson says that marijuana smoking was as common-place in the black urban communities then as it is in the wider American society today – plentiful, and the sex, participatory or spectator, as variable as the imagination. Her niece tells Albertson that Bessie Smith's main activities that night in Detroit were drink-ing and watching the various performances in different rooms of the buffet flat. In a recorded interview with Albertson, released as a track on a collection of gay, lesbian and bisexual blues tracks, *AC/DC Blues*, Ruby described the clientèle as 'nothing but faggots and bulldykers'. I should stress that these to her are merely collo-quial terms, used without any malicious or pejorative tone, and simply as descriptive street slang. She describes one of the main attractions that visit, in a tone of admiration, as a young black man who astonished onlookers with his skill at making love to another man. Describing what she calls a 'tongue bath', she explains, 'when he got to the front of that guy, [the guy] was shakin' like a leaf'. While, again, we have to be careful not to impose modern construc-tions of homosexuality on the black urban American communities in the 1920s, such reports would suggest that homosexuality figured in those communities in a way that the history books and historians have not previously told us.

For a while, Smith was able to keep her lesbian affairs a secret from Jack Gee, but it was only a matter of time before he found out. At one point, a black newspaper gossip column printed a coded allusion to Smith's friendship with male impersonator Gladys Ferguson, warning 'Gladys' to stay away from 'B' because 'G' would get angry. B was Bessie Smith, G was Jack Gee. Luckily for most of those involved, including the author of the piece, neither Smith nor Gee were big newspaper readers. Eventually, Gee did find out, discovering Smith in bed with another young woman, on the same tour as the Detroit buffet flat visit. Smith and her lover fled the room, hiding until Gee left in search of Smith, at which point Smith gathered up her troupe and left town in a hurry, just as she had done on other occasions in her turbulent relationship with Jack Gee.

Clearly, Bessie Smith felt no qualms about her queer love affairs, merely about the likelihood of violent reprisal from a husband who was, anyway, two-timing her and living high on the hog off her earnings. Chris Albertson ascribes this to her lack of social pretensions: where other performers aspired to enter white society circles, Smith was happiest among the people she had grown up with and who had now made her a superstar. Even when transplanted into white society, such as her appearance at a party thrown by bisexual socialite and blues buff Carl Van Vechten, Bessie Smith behaved as Bessie Smith behaved. It is hard to imagine whether she simply declined to play their games or found it impossible to mimic them. Either way, her behaviour bespeaks a powerful, and perhaps unshakeable, sense of self, even if her life was at times chaotic and, in the end, tragic. She died in a road accident in 1937, when another vehicle hit the passenger side of a car in which she was travelling. Columbia began the first re-issues of Smith's work a year later, and re-issues have continued to appear ever since. Her lying-in-state attracted ten thousand mourners, although her grave in a Philadelphia cemetery was left unmarked (Jack Gee stole the money meant for her headstone) until 1970, when Juanita Green, who had known Smith as a child, and singer Janis Joplin paid for a stone to mark the grave.

Smith was by no means the only blues performer to pursue lesbian relationships actively. Her elder and, some say, her mentor, Gertrude 'Ma' Rainey, while also married, found time to explore her lesbian desires. One Rainey tune contains the complaint that people wonder why she is all alone, 'because a sissy shook that thing, and took my man from home'. An incident reported by Chris Albertson (when researching queer blues, all roads seem to lead to Albertson: even contemporary black gay historians and critics end up at Albertson's door) describes a party which Rainey threw for her troupe of young women performers that developed into something approaching a lesbian orgy. Rainey and her friends had been drinking and partying, and made so much noise that a neighbour called the police. When the police arrived, pandemonium ensued as women attempted to dress and flee. Rainey was the last to leave, clutching someone else's dress, and she would have made good her escape had she not fallen down a flight of stairs and then been apprehended. Accusing her of running an indecent party, the police threw her in jail for the night. It was Bessie Smith, hearing about her incarceration, who bailed Rainey the following morning.

Smith and Rainey were by no means the only lesbian blues artists, although owing to the hypocrisy and homophobia of jazz writers (a criticism that is still being levelled by black gay critics in the mid-1990s) much queer blues history has been erased and lost for ever. While individual stories have been censored or elided to gloss over details of oppositional sexuality (historian Eric Garber claims that Gladys Bentley, Jackie Moms Mabley, Alberta Hunter, Josephine Baker and Ethel Waters were also lesbian or bisexual), evidence exists to suggest that homosexuality was both common-place in black society and an acceptable topic for musical treatment in the frequently ribald, and indeed lewd, world of the blues. A recent biography also detailed Billie Holiday's lesbian affairs.

Again, thanks to Chris Albertson, examples of queer blues remain, like twentieth-century Sapphic fragments snatched from the flames of history. The compilation *AC/DC Blues*, a collection of 'gay blues' released in 1977 by the American label Stash, con-tains some fourteen tracks addressing or alluding to gay or lesbian passion. Smith's 'Foolish Man Blues' is included, as is Ma Rainey's far more revealing 'Prove It On Me Blues', in which she admits to dressing like a man to go out with a gang of women friends to places that don't let men in. The company must be female, she insists, ''cause I don't like no men'. Rainey's narrator gets into fights and loses her girl, but even if she is acting wild she defiantly asserts 'ain't nobody caught me, they sure got to prove it on me'. Smith's 'Foolish Man Blues' appears to have been the only song in which the singer referred to queer sex, although her silence on the matter may have been inspired by the fear of revealing her own bisexuality to Jack Gee. Some of the blues on *AC/DC Blues* are baffling to a modern-day English listener (this one, at least), or oblique, or plain blunt; Tampa Red's 'It's Tight Like That', a ris-qué reference to the sundry applications for KY or Crisco, doesn't appear to be gender-specific, and Harlem Ham Fats's 'Garbage Man' employs that profession in a metaphor for anal sex ('stick out your can' being sexual code). Others, however, are quite explicit in their references. 'Boy in the Boat', one of two songs by writer-singer George Hannah accompanied by legendary pianist Meade Lux Lewis, is allusive to gay sexuality but explicit in its references to lesbians – promoting tolerance of women who walk hand in hand, and explaining about women-only parties where they keep the lights down low. Hannah's 'Freakish Man Blues' employs more surreal metaphors for sex than Peter Gabriel's 'Sledge-hammer', and concludes with its narrator apparently thinking that he might be gay. Al Miller's 1936 'Ain't That a Mess' presents a catalogue of incestuous couplings between a permutation of relatives, each of whom is quoted with the refrain, 'didn't mean no harm, just showin' her/him what to do'. Working through the various family members, the song refers to a sister whom mother calls brother, and a little brother who the narrator finds 'teaching daddy what to do, / said he didn't mean no harm, just showin' him what to do'.

Bessie Jackson's 1935 song, 'B.D. Woman's Blues', while appearing to be sung as social observation from a heterosexual perspective, has a sneaking admiration for the subjects it describes. B.D. Women (the initials should be obvious, now as then), Jackson sings, 'ain't gonna need no men'. B.D. Women, she further reports, walk just like natural men, and 'lay their jive just like a natural man'. The song is among the most explicit on the album, and its description of assertive lesbians, particularly in its observation of the fact that they matched men in economic terms, can have left no one in any doubt as to the position of lesbians in the black urban culture of the period.

Perhaps most interesting, however, is a slighter song, no less explicit in its content, but pitched in a way that it could be considered a comical music hall piece. Yet the fact that it has been covered by a number of performers, at least three recorded on *AC/DC Blues*, suggests that the song, 'Sissy Man Blues', had an even wider currency than the listener might imagine. If three versions exist that we know of, then that suggests both that it was a popular title and that others must, surely, have existed, if only in the sense of a folk tune shared by word of mouth. Intriguingly, it also bears a striking resemblance to a 'rich' Scottish folk ditty which I heard as a child, sung by an adult relative two or three whiskies west of his inhibitions. ('Tiddlywinks old man, get a woman if you can, if you can't get a woman get a nice old man.' Sung, moreover, to a sailor's hornpipe reminiscent of 'The Blue Peter'.)

'Sissy Man Blues' opens with the ultimate blues cliché, 'Woke up this morning', although instead of finding the blues all 'round his bed, the narrator finds his 'business' in his hand. In other versions, he wakes up with his 'troubles' in his hand, and his business or troubles often have meat metaphors attached. He has a girl, but she isn't around (in one version, he thinks a venue called the 'Daisy Chain' may hold clues to her whereabouts). If you can't bring or send me a woman, he pleads in each and every version of the song, bring (or send) me a sissy man. On one level, 'Sissy Man Blues' might be read as an act of desperation, but none of the versions on *AC/DC Blues* configures the song that way. If anything, what is most apparent is the narrator's willingness to participate in queer sex as an alternative; his willingness, moreover, to voice that desire. With the rare exception of gender confusion songs (The Kinks' 'Lola', most notably) I cannot think of any white pop songs that have ever roamed into the area of queer sex like this, less still contemplated or even acknowledged it as a positive sexual option.

While they may represent fragmentary and underwhelming evidence of the queer presence in the black urban communities, these songs suggest that male and female homosexuality had a role in black culture at the beginning of the century which has been denied black men and women in the decades since. A number of factors have contributed to this situation. Firstly, much, indeed the vast majority, of the writing about black American music has been produced by white heterosexual males. (I am aware, also, as a white male, that I too am skating on thin ice here, but I can only acknowledge that problematized viewpoint and strive for the impossible, objectivity.) Chris Albertson, in his sleeve notes to *AC/DC Blues*, lays the blame for the erasure of this queer history at the door of jazz critics. 'It is a sad fact,' he writes, 'that most jazz critics – though they should be familiar with the material represented here – will be made uncomfortable by the gay theme of this album; they prefer to believe that homosexuality and jazz are mutually exclusive, or – if they recognize its existence at all – that it is something worse than dope addiction, a shameful skeleton to be kept in the closet.' Pointing out, with quiet but irresistible force, that record buyers would have known exactly what they were purchasing on these recordings, he concludes, 'Perhaps some day lesbian singers will no longer have to sing about the men they never desired, and gay male vocalists will be able to choose or write material they truly can identify with; perhaps, too, jazz writers will learn that the men and women they write about are human beings and not just names on a record label.'

Alas, this is far from the case. Indeed, as we shall see, jazz criticism, as it is practised by white heterosexual males on either side of the Atlantic, is one of the last bastions of intellectualized homophobia, a virulent bigotry which in fact leaks back into a furtive racism, one that allows the white critic the plantation boss's position of power over his subject (and, yes, my ice-skate bootlaces may be unravelling here). In the 1990s, white critics still say things (mostly in private) about black gay performers which would invite prosecution if they were said about blacks in general, or Jews.

Over the years, this has been compounded by the efforts of the aspiring black middle-classes to disown what they perceive as a disreputable, shameful, embarrassing or stereotyping past. This has been driven in part by the Christian church, which has fought to erase African and Caribbean culture from north American black culture. This normalizing or assimilationist programme appears to want to present North American blacks as white folk who just happen to be black. As one black gay writer, Max C. Smith, points out, writing in the black gay anthology *In the Life*, 'The American Black's bias against gays is due to our forced socialization into Dixie Christian culture during slavery. Other African traditions such as polygamy, a close communion with nature, and a strong abhorrence of violence were also systematically terminated by the Dixie slave-owning Christians.' Wherever you find institutionalized black homophobia, you will also find, I believe, powerful fundamentalist religion, be it Christianity or Islam.

The one place where such information about black America's queer heritage might hope to get a fair hearing, before the black intelligentsia, is a site where this knowledge has been constantly betrayed. From the historians of the Harlem Renaissance – who know, as we do, that Langston Hughes was by no means the only gay man in the Renaissance, even though his estate is still trying to censor comment even on Hughes's life – to radical black activists such as Louis Farrakhan, heterosexual black American intellectuals have ignored or denied their homosexual brothers' and sisters' stories. Feminism brought new perspectives to the subject, and as poet and critic Essex Hemphill points out in his introduction to the collection of black gay writing *Brother to Brother*, Black Panther leader Huey Newton once proposed a revolutionary alliance between blacks, gays and feminists. Yet as late as 1991 Hemphill could still complain, in his essay 'Undressing Icons' from that same collection, of 'the practice among black academicians of ignoring gays and lesbians in almost every articulation and theory concerning matters of race and culture'.

This systematic denial of black gay and lesbian culture has filtered down through the eras and genres of black music, and can be seen today in the promotion of homophobic attitudes by some individuals in the reggae and rap worlds. This is something I want to discuss later. In the meantime, I would like to return to the iconic Bessie Smith. I don't know if Smith would have appreciated my journalistic attentions. Her story retains its integrity, regardless, thanks to the attentions of a biographer like Albertson and thanks to her own powerful personality as a black woman who refused to be a victim in a situation where she was not offered any other options. Even if she had to take recourse to her fists, Smith was a woman at the controls of her own destiny. If I had a time machine and the time machine could deposit Bessie Smith in modern-day Kingston, Jamaica, for a confrontation with either Shabba Ranks or Buju Banton, I wouldn't want to be either of those silly boys for all the tea in China.

Chapter five

And His Mother Called Him Bill

'I came up here once,' said Brian, 'to the jazz festival.'
Michael turned and smiled at him. Sterile or
not, this man was breeder through and through. 'Best
of Breeder', he had called him once. Surely there were
gay men somewhere who revered jazz, but Michael
didn't know any.

● Armistead Maupin, *Significant Others*

Strolling down Castro or Polk with my headphones on,
listening to perhaps Ellington, Coltrane, or Gary
Burton, I see hundreds of gay men and wonder if any
of them ever hear such music.

● *Gene Miller, gay jazz DJ, formerly of KJAZ San
Francisco.*

TWO comments from either sides of one coin, written with
entirely different intentions, but speaking to a common myth about
masculine sexuality and jazz which, given the slightest nudge, col-
lapses like a house of cards.

Armistead Maupin, ever the gentle satirist, is scoring a point
off the well-known factoid that gay men don't like jazz (less still
play it) and that for many queers jazz is an irredeemably heterosexual, breeder, pastime. Gene Miller, possibly Armistead Maupin's

neighbour, was actually responding to a 1985 article in an American jazz newsletter which claimed that homosexuals not only don't play/listen to jazz but are incapable of doing so. Miller ended his letter asking if he was the only gay man in the world who listened to Johnny Hodges, Sinatra, Lester Young and Thelonious Monk. (Little did he know it, but he was actually *listening* to at least one and possibly two queers when he walked down Castro or Polk.) But thus does the myth about queers versus jazz persist.

The myth is a hangover from the heyday of bebop fifty years ago, when the image of the jazz musician as Romantic outsider, a fast-living womanizer with an insatiable appetite for alcohol and narcotics, was first established. The myth should have been buried alongside the bebop giants. Most typically, it is based on the life and career of saxophonist Charlie 'Bird' Parker, nicknamed for his flights of inspired playing. The Parker myth, that part of his genius lay in his heroin habit, led countless other players to experiment with and become habituated to heroin, cocaine and lesser drugs. Jazz history is spotted with such legendary, tragic figures, tracking back to the pre-history of jazz and characters like trumpeter Buddy Bolden (the subject of Michael Ondaatje's novel *Coming Through Slaughter*) and up to the present day, when a number of major, mainly white, jazz figures still use heroin. The brilliant young bassist Jaco Pastorius, once a member of Weather Report, who died in 1991, is probably its most recent victim.

These figures, however, are a small minority. The majority of jazz musicians today have mortgages, families and fairly bourgeois values. Substance abuse is probably more common in television and banking than it is in jazz. However, the demonization of substance abuse, like the demonization of sexuality, lets society anaesthetize itself to the fact that millions of people are legally addicted to Halcyon and Prozac. And society won't start to deal with the drug culture until it acknowledges that the vast number of 'drug addicts' are housewives and businessmen.

The sexing of jazz has been conducted – as is common in all cultures – by its historians and critics, and these have, with few exceptions, been heterosexual WASP males with an intellectual agenda to pursue. Jazz became a multi-racial music quite quickly after its birth as 'jass' or 'jasz' (like the later 'rock'n'roll', black slang for fucking), a hybrid of ragtime and New Orleans dance-hall/brothel tunes. Whites latched on to it, as they did to rock'n'-roll in the 1950s and, to a lesser extent, to roots reggae in the 1970s, because it was a rebel noise that thrilled as much as it appalled the establishment. Owing to segregation, white jazz developed in tandem with but separate to black jazz. As in rock'n'-roll, whites often borrowed black innovations and toned them down for domestic consumption. Then as now, heterosexual WASP critics called the shots, and then as now heterosexual WASP critics policed the public images of their heroes. The British critic Max Jones, for example, took a whole library of unrepeatable anecdotes about Billie Holiday, among others, to his grave. Similarly, British and American critics have appointed themselves as security guards outside the closets of many jazz artists living and dead. Just as it took a candid observer like Humphrey Carpenter to address Britten's sexuality, it took an unusually sympathetic writer like Chris Albertson to consider that of Bessie Smith, and so far Albertson is in a field of his own. The sexuality of jazz musicians, black or white, is often 'not relevant' to a musician's life, or dismissed as a peccadillo, something on a par with a minor hobby or food fad. Quite often, this is done to protect the HWASPCs from their own unresolved fears about sexuality – HWASPCs are not noted for their emotional maturity; some might even say it's a condition of the job – and it is possible that the urge to edit and suppress information about a musician's sexuality may also be linked to unresolved tensions about race.

As anyone who reads Albertson's book on Smith will discover, homosexuality was a commonplace, if not particularly widespread, among the black urban communities at the beginning of this century. American gay historian Jonathan Ned Katz, in his mammoth *Gay American History*, tracks examples of socialized homosexuality among slaves and free blacks which go back hundreds of years. The era of Freud and the naming of homosexuality ushered in a culture of quite persistent denial, by the black middle classes as well as white, to the extent that anyone approaching the sexuality of a jazz musician finds themselves committing what would be akin to an act of slander were the subject still alive. (Indeed, as the Jason Donovan versus *The Face* débâcle proved, accusing someone of being dishonest about their alleged homosexuality can be libellous in Britain.) This information is never passive or neutral, it comes armed. It is a claim, an allegation, an accusation. It never describes, it exposes.

With musicians themselves under pressure, real or imagined, to keep their sexuality a secret, it's no surprise that writers like Maupin can get away with their mischievous jokes. Maupin's jesting is, of course, benign, but there is a subtext to the wider argument which seems to subscribe to a grotesque stereotyping: who'd imagine, the myth seems to say, an effeminate poof listening to, for example, Duke Ellington, or Dexter Gordon, less still Cecil Taylor, or Sun Ra's Space Arkestra. Boy do I have news for them!

Homosexuality, or rumour of homosexuality, for any sense of 'gay pride' has a snowball's chance in hell in such an atmosphere, has been a sub rosa topic in jazz since its beginnings. Perhaps the earliest rumours, which continue to circulate today, involved the unhappy private life of brilliant young cornettist Bix Beiderbecke. Born into a comfortable Mid-West German émigré family, the precociously gifted Beiderbecke was entranced by the early jazz music he heard on the Mississippi steamers that passed through his Iowa home town of Davenport. He learnt the cornet by listening to jazz records on a wind-up gramophone, and proved to have an uncannily natural ear. He was playing on the riverboats by his mid-teens, and made a name for himself as a superb if unconventional player before his twenties. He joined the famous Paul Whiteman Orchestra, but was dead at twenty-eight from the cumulative effects of alcoholism, which had manifested itself during his college days. Despite youthful high jinks, Beiderbecke appears to have been a polite and shy young man, who made only half-hearted attempts at dating girls, and from the reports of his biographers seemed to enjoy the company of his fellow musicians. Certainly, nothing 'untoward', as their terminology would no doubt dub it, is recorded in any of the books about Beiderbecke, but then again we would not expect it to be. Yet as recently as 1994, I found this rumour still circulating, and in politically credible circles, related to me by a liberal, left-leaning and jazz-loving gay man.

The first actual out gay jazz musician I've come across so far is Wilbur Ware, a bassist with the Count Basie big band in the 1950s. Conversations a musician friend has had on the New York black music scene suggest that Ware was self-identified as homosexual among his colleagues, that he was happy for them to know he was a homosexual and that they were happy to have an out homosexual on the bandstand with them. Considering jazz's background in the whorehouse and buffet flat, this shouldn't necessarily be so surprising; in fact, the surprise might be that more gay men did not follow Ware's example. Again, it is difficult to imagine the lifestyle of a black homosexual in America during the 1940s and 1950s, and even documentaries like *Before Stonewall* concentrate on the white experience in those years. Like those of most of his counterparts, Ware's life would be a hectic and sometimes punishing round of rehearsing, touring, recording, with a private life fitted into the brief time off between these activities. Yet given the tenor of the times, it is remarkable that Ware should feel confident to live as openly homosexual as he did, although it is equally likely that the brutality of racism in America actually kept black homosexuals from the public eye.

The most persistent rumour, and one confirmed in 1987 with the publication of James Lincoln Collier's biography of Duke Ellington, is that involving Duke Ellington's longtime (1939–67) collaborator, deputy pianist and arranger, Billy Strayhorn. For decades, Strayhorn was Ellington's right-hand man and the composer of some of the most ravishing music the Ellington big band ever performed. Interestingly, it seems to be acknowledged among most liberal jazz musicians that Strayhorn was indeed gay. (There are even suggestions, from respectable sources, that Ellington himself was probably bisexual.)

Strayhorn was born in Dayton, Ohio, in 1915, to a comfortable middle-class black family, and displayed musical abilities at an early age. By the time he was in high school, Strayhorn was considered 'an intellectual and a dandy', according to Collier, with a taste for smart clothes. Bizarrely, Strayhorn was already reading *The New Yorker* while still in high school. He even staged a number of musical revues in high school, although as yet he wasn't interested in jazz. Then one day, he saw the Ellington orchestra perform at high school, and was hooked. He began experimenting with his own compositions and arrangements, forming bands with friends to play his own material, and studying arrangement. A friend urged him to approach Ellington, and at a Pittsburgh concert by the Ellington orchestra Strayhorn went backstage and introduced himself, showing Ellington some of his work. Strayhorn was barely into his twenties, but the material he showed Ellington included 'Lush Life', which would become a classic. Recognizing the young man's talent, Ellington invited Strayhorn to visit him whenever he made it to New York.

Strayhorn showed up in New York shortly after this meeting, and Ellington quickly found him work in the organization that surrounded his band. Soon, Strayhorn was arranging for small group combos in the orchestra, and taking rehearsal sessions. Ellington began to rely on Strayhorn as his musical assistant, although the role might better be described as musical director.

As James Lincoln Collier points out, the arrival of this kid, still barely into his twenties and relatively inexperienced, could have inspired great jealousy among the old hands of the Ellington orchestra. Instead, it seems, they adopted him, in the nearest popular analogy I can muster, as a sort of Radar to their M*A*S*H 4077. An early photograph of Ellington and Strayhorn playing the piano together resembles a black equivalent of Radar and Colonel Henry Potter playing 'Chopsticks' together. Strayhorn was barely 5 foot 3 inches tall, clamped behind thick black-framed spectacles, shy and unassertive but friendly and good-natured. These various qualities won him the affectionate nickname of Sweetpea, after Olyve Oyl's accident-prone baby in the Popeye cartoons, and it is clear from the countless effusive tributes to him that the Ellington band doted on Strayhorn and came to admire his work as well.

Strayhorn's relationship with Ellington was rather more complex, although the same could be said of the bandleader's relationship with the majority of the people in his life. Ellington was born into a middle-class black family that instilled Victorian bourgeois values in all its children. The nickname Duke, in fact, was inspired by his often imperious behaviour as a child. This was in part a tactic of the black emancipation movement, conducting oneself in so impeccable a manner as to shame the white power elite, but at times it was also plain and simple snobbery. Ellington subscribed to a social order that made him reluctant to invite some members of his band into his own home because of their social background and manners. When the Ellington band became famous and its leader wealthy, Ellington travelled first class while the band travelled third, the bandleader checking into white-only hotels that readily greeted the celebrity Ellington while the band had to find accommodation elsewhere. (He was, however, neither the first nor the last bandleader to do this.)

Like many a genius, Ellington was also a user of people. Observers quoted by Collier and other biographers frequently use the word 'love' when describing Strayhorn's emotional and creative devotion to Ellington. Ellington's feelings for him were almost as strong. One close friend described Strayhorn as one of the four most (and perhaps only) important people in Ellington's life, along with his mother and sister, although excluding all of his wives and mistresses. One friend described Ellington as a 'devourer' of relationships. He certainly relied on Strayhorn to support him beyond the call of duty for nigh on thirty years.

A glance at the composer credits on any Ellington album – like many a jazz album, and many pop recordings since – can be deceptive. Where Ellington is credited for the vast bulk of his output, it is widely accepted, as Collier says, that when we hear Ellington's work for the great part we are also hearing the work of Billy Strayhorn. As well as arranging Ellington's material, Strayhorn also contributed ideas, themes, melodies, and sometimes entire tunes. There is at least one instance, and possibly many more, of an original piece of sheet music for a famous Ellington tune which has Strayhorn's name and chosen title crossed out and Ellington's own name and title inscribed above.

Members of Strayhorn's family have said that had he worked harder he would have become a famous composer in his own right, and considering his likely input into the Ellington canon this is probably true. Strayhorn was, however, rather lazy, and easily diverted. He would sooner be out partying with friends – among them Lena Horne, the original voice of 'Stormy Weather', first in *Cabin in the Sky*, then in the film *Stormy Weather* – than composing, and became notorious for deadline surfing. When all the pros and cons are added up, the Strayhorn–Ellington relationship probably balances out at a happy if haphazard symbiosis.

Strayhorn's first big break with the Ellington band came in early 1940, when Ellington was virtually taken off air by America's radio stations in a battle with the copyright protection agency, ASCAP, the American Society of Composers and Publishers, its equivalent to Britain's Performing Right Society. ASCAP wanted to increase the charges it levied for radio performances of music registered with ASCAP. The radio stations countered by banning all ASCAP music from the airwaves, and also launched their own copyright protection agency, BMI, Broadcast Music Incorporated. As luck would have it, Ellington was an ASCAP member, Strayhorn a BMI member. For a short while, until the dispute was resolved, Ellington was forced to use Strayhorn's material in his radio broadcasts (as well as that of his son and amanuensis, Mercer Ellington).

Among the Strayhorn pieces featured in the Ellington repertoire at this time were the rarity 'Charpoy', recorded on the Strayhorn tribute album, *And His Mother Called Him Bill*, the more famous Ellington standard, 'Chelsea Bridge', and perhaps one of the most famous titles in the history of jazz, 'Take the A Train'. Strayhorn gave the tune that title out of simple civic-mindedness: a new subway tunnel was being dug running from central Manhattan north through Harlem, and many people were finding their journeys disrupted or diverted because of the building work. The simplest way around the problem, as Strayhorn advised, was to take the A train.

As a queer jazz fan, I have to confess a certain glee, pride, smugness and delight that so famous a jazz tune as 'Take the A Train' was written by a homo. It is one of the handful of jazz tunes that virtually everybody has either heard or knows by its title. It's up there with ''Round Midnight', 'Night in Tunisia' and 'In the Mood'. It is also one of the most easily recognized jazz tunes in history, more than 'Straight No Chaser' or 'String of Pearls'. Millions of people are carrying this queer jazz tune around in their memory, unawares, and one can only imagine their reaction were they to be informed of its queer provenance.

The Strayhorn story by no means stops there. Until his death from cancer in 1967, Strayhorn was a vital component in the Ellington band, as composer, arranger and deputy pianist. The reach of his influence on Ellington's work is difficult and perhaps impossible to estimate, but it certainly includes most of the classic Ellington tunes and a great many of his jazz suites as well. In some ways, although younger than Ellington, Strayhorn was his intellectual superior, trained in music, conversant with the modern classical music that was often invoked by Ellington's critical admirers, better read and artistically attuned than Ellington, who often used his hauteur to mask his ignorance of contemporary artistic matters.

Whether Sweetpea was credited or not, it is clear that when we listen to the breathtaking architecture of Ellington's music, it is Strayhorn we admire as the architect, even though Ellington was the original conceptualist and the designer who put his final touch to the architecture. Strayhorn's unquantifiable input into Ellington's work rather undermines the adjectival compliment 'Ellingtonian' that has been bandied about ever since, although a postmodernist might argue that 'Duke Ellington' is a fictional collaboration between Sweetpea and Edward Kennedy Ellington. This is not to deny Ellington's own input into his work, rather to hope that one might slightly redress the balance in favour of the composer who stayed backstage when Ellington wanted the limelight. At the very least, Strayhorn's style contributes a rarefied grace to Ellington's work that is sometimes missing from the pieces written after Strayhorn's death.

Strayhorn contributed enough major pieces to the Ellington orchestra canon, anyway, from 'Lush Life' to 'Blood Count', which Strayhorn wrote while he was in hospital dying of cancer, and which contains moments of blues melancholy as sublime as Charles Mingus's 'Goodbye Pork Pie Hat'. If we were to apply the literary notion of intertextuality here – the idea that an earlier text can feed its essences into and through later texts, by influence, allusion or direct quotation by the later author – then we could say that Ellington and his queer sidekick are still making themselves heard in every good jazz record and performance since 1940 and up until the music that we now call jazz dies out.

Sweetpea's sexuality is probably all but lost to the secrecy and misguided discretion of his friends and acquaintances. James Lincoln Collier records it almost as though hoping the careless reader might not notice it. In the few pages he devotes to a brief biographical note on Strayhorn, Collier comments that in his teens Strayhorn was 'somewhat unself-assertive; and it is clear that his homosexuality was already developing at this point in his life.' Collier gives no indication of what might have made Strayhorn's homosexuality 'clear', nor does he refer to it ever again in his book. It is almost as though Collier felt he could not avoid mentioning Strayhorn's queerness but wished to state it and then flee on into his text, like someone in a game of pass the parcel who suddenly finds a bomb in their hands. It also seems likely that Collier finds Strayhorn's homosexuality problematical, possibly because he is addressing a primarily American audience.

We might not have access to the details of Sweetpea's queer lifestyle, but we might mine a few useful clues from the evidence scattered about the Ellington story. Importantly, Strayhorn appears to have been a universally loved, indeed, adored figure in the Ellington camp, an affection matched by the respect his skills as composer and arranger commanded. Something from later in his life also resounds in our attempt to get a take on the personality of Billy Strayhorn. His death coincided with Ellington's preparations for the second of his now-legendary Sacred Music concerts. One of the pieces in this concert, 'Freedom', involved the choir reciting Strayhorn's own personal philosophical credo, which in the circumstances is both remarkable and tremendously moving. These were the four freedoms that Billy Strayhorn strived to live by: 'freedom from hate unconditionally; freedom from self-pity; freedom from the fear of doing something that would help someone else more than it does me; and freedom from the kind of pride that makes me feel I am better than my brother'.

Recorded the year before the assassination of civil rights leader Martin Luther King, by which time Strayhorn was dead, these words shine with the rhetoric of the 1960s civil rights movement, but they also echo in tune with the rhetoric of Stonewall and the birth of gay liberation. Considering these fragments of evidence about a life we will probably never really know about, I can't help wondering if there isn't a house somewhere in Dayton, Ohio, that is missing a plaque in memory of Billy Strayhorn, Genius, Queer Saint.

Chapter six

Miles in the Sky

QUEERS have continued to enter the field of jazz since the death of Billy Strayhorn, of course, just as many of us have continued to listen to jazz. (One of the things that prompted me to write this book was the number of gay men I saw in the audience of a Chick Corea concert in London in the early 1990s.) They are not, perhaps, numerous, but as the culture of denial continues, with little or no sign of abating, it is important that we track and tag these queers before they disappear for ever.

It is often the case that their homosexuality is little more than rumour, because the dominant culture refuses to negotiate this information on any other basis, and because the individuals themselves are reluctant to go public with what they fear may be damaging information. Neither side is wholly silent on the matter, however. These people – meaning, by and large, gay men – are not wholly closeted, but pursue a queer lifestyle in a clandestine fashion. Nor are the people – critics, promoters, label owners – whose livelihoods might be threatened by this information entirely quiescent on the subject. They discuss the homosexuality of certain jazz musicians among themselves, gossip and dish, to the extent that this talk becomes the instrument of oppression itself, the act by which these people are silenced. Thus the hearsay evidence that the late Dexter Gordon was probably bisexual will be buried for ever. Thus bandleader Sun Ra wasn't 'really' queer because he 'never' had sex (how on earth did they know?). And thus, according to one eminent American critic, Cecil Taylor, that colossus of modern jazz, allegedly can't play the piano 'properly' (!) because he's a queer. While the subjects of this Burroughsian viral chatter attempt to maintain a dignified silence on what is being constructed as a sort of psychic disfigurement, those with access to this 'in the know' information play fast and loose with the most intimate details of their private lives. In America in the 1980s, there was a great furore over the case of Michael Hardwick, whose home was raided by police officers looking for evidence that he had committed the 'crime' of homosexual sex. The gay media made much of the notion of 'letting the police into Michael Hardwick's bedroom'. We might similarly ask when did the jazz press plant spies in Sun Ra's bedroom, and when did critic Stanley Crouch take up his surveillance position at the bottom of Cecil Taylor's bed?

This information can be yours for the price of a beer. Buy a jazz critic a drink and most of them will happily out any number of closeted jazz musicians for you. They will not sympathize with the subject, nor will they regret that the subject is or was unable to come out as queer. The commonest accompanying sound is a chuckle, as though the subject's queerness were, yet again, just some amusing little peccadillo. This is how I first heard about Sun Ra, from the slyly homophobic jazz critic Brian Case, who also supplied the additional information that some members of his Arkestra are/were probably gay too. We might consider the insiders who have and wield this information as blackmailers who demand and get something vastly more expensive than money – silence.

Herman 'Sonny' Blount, Sun Ra or, as he referred to himself in the years before his death, Le Sony Ra, went along with the blackmailers' demands for decades. As Herman Blount, he began his career as a pianist and arranger with the Fletcher Henderson big band, when Henderson's band vied with the Ellington orchestra for the title of greatest jazz big band in America. In the 1950s, Blount transformed himself into Sun Ra, his big band into the Arkestra (or Space Arkestra, or Solar Myth Arkestra; the variations were endless) producing a stream of seriously wigged out space-jazz albums employing electric keyboards and, later, synthesizers to produce sounds that prefigured the electronic experiments of the Pink Floyd and German experimental bands like Can. Ra constructed an entire mythology about himself, and his band, claiming, among other things, to be a deity from outer space. On a good day, Ra and his

Arkestra were never less than stunning, dressed in what looked like cast-offs from early episodes of *Star Trek*, mixing virtuoso 1940s big band arrangements, ritual percussion extravaganzas (complete with dances and marches), scorching improvised passages, howling noise workouts and swinging massed chants ('space is the place', 'along came Ra'). Shortly before his death, they even recorded an entire album of famous Disney tunes. If, as the queer writer and painter Brion Gysin once claimed, 'Mankind is here to go' into outer space, then Sun Ra and his Arkestra were here to give us a rousing send-off.

American director Robert Mugge's 1980 film, *Sun Ra: A Joyful Noise*, an hour-long documentary about Ra's band, life and work, filmed the Arkestra live atop a Philadelphia skyscraper and explored the band's links with the local black community. Members of the Arkestra lived in a commune, following a rota of domestic chores as well as a punishing schedule of daily rehearsal. In many ways, life in Sun Ra's Arkestra resembled that in a monastery. The Arkestra was also involved in outreach work with the local black community, assisting education projects, food co-ops and the like. Live, there was always something ineffably camp about the band; on that Philadelphia skyscraper, Ra in spacey robes and what looks like his mum's tea-cosy on his head, the band themselves dolled up in a variety of Egypto-Martian outfits, Ra and Arkestra looked like they were waiting to be picked up by the mothership from *Close Encounters*, but it was the uncompromising force of the band's playing, and the strength of soloists like saxophonists John Gilmore and Marshall Allen, that prevented the Arkestra from lapsing into hilarity or farce. And when Sun Ra rapped about his mythology and about his origins in outer space, you were left with the suspicion, well, what if he was right?

As with the case of John Cage, it is saddening to think that Sun Ra could be out about so many things — not least his regal ancient Egyptian ancestors, and the fact that he didn't come from this planet — but not about his sexual orientation. And there seems to be something pernicious about the fact that the bush telegraph of rumour should be discussing whether or not Sun Ra ever had queer sex, and whether or not the claim that he 'never' had sex meant that he wasn't 'really' queer. Somewhere inside that warped reasoning is someone who desperately doesn't want Herman Blount to be proved homosexual. The argument resembles an appeal to some external authority to decide on Blount's non-homosexuality. He didn't 'do it', the argument claims, so he couldn't really have been one. (The argument also tidily overlooks the fact that even if he didn't 'do it', if Sonny had jerk-off fantasies about, say, Sidney Poitier or Bill Cosby, he was still a queer.)

In fact, the 'argument' about Sun Ra, if we can find it in ourselves to give this sad, crazy perversion of logic the status of reasoned debate, springs from a profound fear of the it which the petitioners claim Sonny didn't do. It, and it alone, seals Herman Blount's fate as either a queer or a non-queer, or, borrowing from the world of physics, antiqueer. It, of course, is fucking, which to the petitioners represents the instant and automatic unmanning of the antiqueer. Whoever formulated this line of 'reasoning', and I'm reluctant to address the topic without employing those apostrophic outriders, needs psychiatric help.

Sadly, even middle-class liberals are sometimes hoodwinked by these acrobatic displays of unreason. Sun Ra died and was buried, as you may have suspected by now, a plump elderly heterosexual in a Mardi Gras frock, and the queer Herman Blount was duly Disappeared in the obituary columns. The talk about him and It died down, but it is still going on around the bush telegraph, like a background hum. And they, whoever They are, this Pynchon-esque agency dedicated to the remanning of famous queers, are still out there, touting that selfsame line. The last person I heard it from, Goddess help us, was a dyke.

The case of Cecil Taylor is even worse than the case of Sun Ra, not least because Taylor is in fact out, but most of all because a wholly dubious pseudo-scientific theory is being used to damn Taylor's sexuality and his creativity. Where the did-he/didn't-he arguments over what Sun Ra did with his dick are, at the end of the day, plain silly, there is something disturbing about this attempt to link Taylor's sexuality with his art. Not only does it hark back to eugenics, I don't think it would be too outlandish to say that it also harks back to the laboratories of Joseph Mengele. The homemade psychology of the theory holds that Taylor is 'unable' to play the piano 'properly' because of his homosexuality, the subtext being that as a queer Taylor is emotionally crippled, retarded, perverted, denatured, aberrant, wrong, *bad*. The perspicacious reader may notice that it has taken some four decades for this factoid to make itself apparent to those who hold this opinion.

Others, and I have to nail my colours to their mast, consider Taylor to be an elemental force in modern music, a Mount Rushmore figure in the history of modern and free jazz, and a composer and pianist whose work invites metaphors from the worlds of seismology and vulcanology.

Stanley Crouch has a point in one, purely technical, sense: Cecil Taylor does have a problem playing the piano. While it is his chosen instrument, Taylor's career has been one long battle to make the instrument produce the noises he wants it to make. Educated at the New England Conservatoire of Music, Taylor brought an awareness of contemporary classical music to the African-American tradition of Ellington, Thelonious Monk and John Coltrane. While acknowledging his immersion in jazz tradition, it is also worthwhile considering Taylor's work in the light of John Cage's invention of the prepared piano and, more interesting still, Conlon Nancarrow's compositions for player piano, an instrument that Nancarrow turned to out of frustration with what eight fingers and two thumbs could do on eighty-eight piano keys. And what Nancarrow needs between eleven and eighty-eight keys to do, Taylor produces on his own during pyrotechnic improvised performances which may also involve dance, song, poetry and movement. For at least three decades, Taylor has been at the forefront of the American avant-garde, and has been showered with accolades and awards, from invitations to the White House from Jimmy Carter, to an award from the prestigious MacArthur Foundation. He has also been singled out as a notoriously difficult performer, and perhaps more than anyone else he has been used by the old guard to symbolize all that is excessive and wrong about the new guard.

It wasn't always so. Taylor's first album, *In Transition*, recorded in 1955, contained covers of Thelonious Monk's 'Bemsha Swing', Ellington's 'Azure', and Cole Porter's 'You'd Be So Nice to Come Home To'. Admittedly, he does take the Porter tune for a walk around the piano, but this is still an album by a musician straddling his heritage and his own future. He followed that album with *Love for Sale*, on which he covered that Porter tune and two others, 'Get Out of Town' and 'I Love Paris', although by this time the improvising demon that would typify Taylor's later work was beginning to show itself. 'I Love Paris' begins with a few recognizable shards of the Porter tune, but uses it as a launch pad into a discursive improvisation around and beyond the original.

Shortly after these two mid- and late-1950s albums, Cecil Taylor cut loose altogether, forming his Unit for such epochal avant-garde albums as *Unit Structures*, and embarking on solo recordings and performances that stunned listeners with the ferocity of their invention and the stamina involved, both for the bravura technique and for the effort involving much of the upper body in playing the piano. Poll awards and the adulation of the hipper critics have pursued Taylor throughout his career, although you sense in some of his press statements that he regrets, with some bitterness, that mainstream acclaim, and mainstream commercial success, have been placed off limits to an artist as uncompromising as he is.

For all his avant-garde notoriety, Taylor is actually a very accessible performer, as later recordings like the hat Hut release, *It Is in the Brewing Luminous*, show. The forearm wallops, elbow stabs and pounding fists that his early critics leapt on, suggesting that one could achieve a similar musical effect working with a jackhammer, belie the sensitivity, intelligence and alertness to his instrument and to his fellow musicians that Taylor displays. Considering his career, it is easier to consider calling Taylor a genius than it would be, say, Keith Jarrett, even if Jarrett's *Köln Concert* is a coffee table favourite. The only Jarrett recording to approach the intensity of Taylor's work is his 1992 album, *Vienna*. There is a brief moment on that album – recorded, perhaps tellingly, shortly after Jarrett had recorded some Shostakovich pieces – where a few simple but devastating chords seem to suggest that Jarrett has glimpsed the end of the universe. By his own admission, this is the first time that Jarrett has touched this 'fire', as he calls it. Cecil Taylor has been playing this fire throughout his career.

So is this what out queer jazz sounds like? Not quite, although it is tempting to equate Taylor's rebellious artistic stance with his sexuality. However, much of this material predates Taylor's public acknowledgements of his sexuality. It has been a non-negotiable fact among his fellow jazz musicians for many years, and has been well known among critics and promoters. When he tours Britain, Taylor has been known to ask tour managers to identify gay bars and other gay venues on the road. In 1985, he gave an interview to a Bay Area newspaper in San Francisco in which he discussed his career in terms of his race and his sexuality being inextricably interlinked as issues. So far, however, no critic or journalist has broached Taylor's sexuality in print, although, as is often the case, most who know of it are perfectly happy to bandy it about among themselves as the luxury of privileged information enjoyed only by those in the know, masonic initiates in this squalid and hypocritical conspiracy of silence. It actually grows to resemble a sort of sexual imperialism, or colonialism, in which these arbiters of information and taste know better than the queer jazz musicians, black or white, who are regarded, really, as little more than plantation darkies.

Perhaps the most explosive rumour about queers in jazz will probably remain just a secret for many years to come, and for solely commercial reasons: the estate of the bisexual trumpeter and composer Miles Davis zealously protects its copyright in the intellectual assets of Davis's life, work and career. No one will corroborate Davis's bisexuality. Claims that Davis died of AIDS-related illness, picked up by British tabloids from publications on the continent, which have different attitudes to and laws governing such disclosure, have gone unproven. Officially, Davis died of pneumonia, stroke and heart failure, a combination which is fairly common among people in the terminal stage of *Pneumocystis carinii* pneumonia (PCP). AIDS diagnoses do not always make it on to death certificates, anyway, often for compassionate reasons. If Davis did die of AIDS-related illnesses, it is just as likely that he contracted HIV in other ways than unprotected sex. For many years he had been a drug user, and we might expect that some of this drug use would have been intravenous. During his 1980s comeback, Davis was said to have cleaned up his act, although this is at variance with backstage gossip on at least the *Decoy* tour. Similarly, in the last decades of his life Davis underwent a number of major operations, some stemming from a car accident in the 1970s, during which he might have contracted HIV from infected blood or blood products. He might also have been kidnapped by Martians and injected with it. Until those who are in possession of the facts about his death release this information, it is equally as likely that he might have contracted HIV from any of the many young male lovers he is said to have had.

In any case, morally and materially, how Miles Davis died should not concern us, although the macabre coincidence of media claims that he died of AIDS-related illness lends chilling if circumstantial evidence to the suggestion that he was bisexual. How Miles Davis lived, however, can legitimately concern us: if the genius responsible for *Kind of Blue*, *Sketches of Spain*, *In a Silent Way*, *Bitches Brew*, *Decoy* and *Tutu* was bisexual, then I think we have another queer saint on our hands, and one who is long overdue canonization. There are enough jazz musicians walking around on either side of the Atlantic who believe, to quote one, that Davis had 'a whole string of young boyfriends', that I for one am convinced that the 'Picasso of jazz' was queer.

This information is hearsay and rumour, at very best vehemently off the record, often because the sources do not wish to appear to be casting a slur on the reputation of the dead trumpeter. Some would argue that this reluctance to acknowledge that dead queers were indeed queer automatically casts a slur on the reputation of every living queer, but most live queers have had to get used to this quirk of second-class citizenry.

The Miles Davis story is a particularly virulent case of this. In periodical journalism at least, Davis rarely had critics as such, rather squadrons of adoring hagiographers. There were the few brave souls who criticized the odd album for being too samey or pop-oriented, and there were also of course the stick-in-the-muds who, like the pre-electric Dylan fans, thought that the world ended the day Davis went electric. These were and still are no match for the thronging membership of the We Love Miles Club, for whom the late trumpeter could do no wrong. I hovered on the edges of the WLMC for a few decades, and still consider some Davis recordings and live shows as the most sublime music I will probably ever hear in my lifetime. I began to peel out of formation at the dull covers of constipated Scritti Politti tunes, and that dumb Cindi Lauper ditty.

But (A. Maupin take note) I revere *Kind of Blue* and *In a Silent Way* like no other albums, jazz or otherwise, and there was a moment in one of Davis's 1980s comeback tour appearances in London when, even from the gods of the Hammersmith Odeon, I felt my skin prickling with awe at the events on stage.

Unlike the WLMC, however, I don't keep Miles Davis down the front of my trousers. More than any other jazz figure, Davis has become inextricably intertwined with the masculine self-image of his admiring chroniclers, to the extent that any questioning of his sexual identity becomes, by extension, a questioning of their sexual identity. Heterosexual male WASP critics are as likely to out Miles Davis as they are to out themselves. Even the most liberal of them become distinctly uneasy when the subject of Davis's sexuality is broached, and this extends to those for whom Davis's bisexuality is a given.

Davis cultivated an image of himself that defined hipster cool; fast cars, beautiful women, sharp clothes, fuck-off-and-die hauteur. Davis's sleeve notes to his soundtrack album, *A Tribute to Jack Johnson*, hymned the late boxer's flamboyant lifestyle; women, cars, champagne and a pet leopard Johnson took walkies in Paris while admiring crowds followed him around. The women were (as in the case of Davis's own dalliance with Juliette Greco) often white, and it is impossible to differentiate this romantic attachment from the fact that Davis clearly saw it as an in-your-face anti-racist statement. Like Johnson, Davis had reasons aplenty for this. There is an iconic photograph of the trumpeter, in a drop-dead cool suit, being led, stumbling, along a street by a policeman, blood pouring from a head wound administered by the cop's nightstick. Davis's only crime was to be seen accompanying a white woman in the street. The cop took this as an invitation to hospitalize the trumpeter. Davis's rarefied macho was more than a shield, it was also a weapon against racism. Unfortunately, Davis came to wield this weapon indiscriminately, although his is neither the first nor the last instance of what some have described as a masculinity impacted by the weight of racism. There have been suggestions that Davis might have been a 'reverse racist', although the line-ups of his bands from the 1960s onwards suggest otherwise: no reverse racist would have peopled his band with so many white and non-black musicians.

Unfortunately, such fastidious myth-making, from his masculinity through his use of language down to his choice of stage clothes, rather militated against a figure such as Davis ever admitting that he was any less heterosexual than his hero Jack Johnson. It seems likely that he took a conscious decision to edit this side of his life from his public image, and that he took this decision even though a number of other options could have been open to him.

One particular option, which I feel is rather poignant, is that Davis might have taken a leaf from his good friend James Baldwin's book(s). Baldwin saw no way, and no reason, to compartmentalize his sexuality away from his racial identity, and saw no alternative but to defend both together. During their long friendship, they must surely have discussed this. The writer Caryl Phillips, in his *The European Tribe*, records a stay with Baldwin in the south of France, during which time Davis visited for an evening. Madly, Phillips hid in his room for the entire evening, terrified at the prospect of being in the same room as James Baldwin and Miles Davis. Phillips writes that the two men talked late into the night, and the shyness of Baldwin's house-guest can have had only limited conversational scope.

Davis could have chosen to embrace his sexuality in the radical agenda – reinventing jazz at least three or four times, flaunting his racial difference in a society he saw symbolized by the Ku-Klux-Klan – which he pursued throughout his life. Instead he chose to take his myth to the grave intact; well, as intact as an ostrich's perception that when it sticks its head in the sand no one can see it. And those who had mortgaged their own hipness against the Davis legend – the writer Richard Williams, for example, who invented a semiology of (heterosexual) cool to decode the green shirt Davis wore on the cover of the 1958 album, *Milestones* – cheered him on into this fraudulent heterosexual mythology. That isn't just sad. It's criminal.

Chapter seven

Two Live Ones: Gary and Graham

THE extent to which subtle and ingrained homophobia is at work in the music industry, the media and the jazz scene, can be measured by an event from the 1980s in which I myself was a minor player. At the time, the episode seemed merely baffling, although in hindsight it is symptomatic of something far larger, and far more pernicious.

In 1983, my partner, Graham Collier, the British jazz composer, musician, writer and educationalist, was asked to write the festival commission for that year's Bracknell Jazz Festival. Held in July in a marquee and tents around the idyllic grounds of South Hill Park Arts Centre outside Bracknell, Hertfordshire, this was Britain's premier modern and contemporary jazz festival until it folded in 1987. Often blessed with glorious weather, this three-day festival drew performers from around the world. The festival commission, supported with funds from the Arts Council, was traditionally seen as a prize, usually reserved for homegrown talent, and intended to give them the support to produce a piece that they might not normally be able to write or stage.

Graham decided to write a lengthy piece for a large band, entitled *Hoarded Dreams*, the hoarded dream being a big band featuring some of his favourite musicians from around Europe and America. The line-up included former Mingus trumpeter Ted Curson, guitarist Terje Rypdal, virtuoso East German trumpeter Conrad Bauer, saxophonist John Surman and many others. The piece was written with the specific qualities of these particular performers in mind, and was intended to showcase their skills improvising together around passages designed to bring out those abilities. In a sense, the piece, clocking in at over an hour, was an aural adventure playground designed for a dozen or so of the finest contemporary and improvising jazz musicians around. Channel 4 expressed interest in making a film of the piece as the core of a documentary about Graham.

Graham was the first British musician to study at the prestigious Berklee College of Music in Boston, back in the 1960s. While serving in the army as a band musician, he won a *down beat* magazine scholarship to Berklee. Returning to London in the mid-1960s, he became part of the new generation of young British jazz musicians, a contemporary of Mike Westbrook, Mike Gibbs and others. At various times, his band has included some of the cream of British jazz players, and has been called a 'nursery' for British talent. He was instrumental in founding Loose Tubes, withdrawing when the big band developed its own leaders. In 1989 he was asked to develop a jazz studies degree course at the Royal Academy of Music in London, which he still directs.

Graham has been out as gay since before the 1967 Sexual Offences Act was passed. His band is probably the only jazz band to have played a gay rights conference, CHE Sheffield 1974, in Britain at least. We met in 1976, when as a rock fan beginning to explore jazz I had already heard his music. We also discovered a shared interest in the work of Malcolm Lowry.

We have been as out a gay couple as we might reasonably expect to be. Family, friends, colleagues and neighbours know about our sexuality, simply as we feel disinclined to conceal it. When the mood takes us, we kiss hello and goodbye at bus stops, stations and airports, and after all these years can only presume that our behaviour together in public must signify 'couple'. We couldn't pass for blokes if we tried. Naturally, we were pleased when, by pure coincidence, the director and producer of the proposed Channel 4 film both turned out to be gay men.

Although the performance of *Hoarded Dreams* was to take up most of the film, the director also wanted footage of Graham at work and interviews with musicians, critics (Brian Priestley, Charles Fox – Britain's greatest jazz critic, now dead, and probably gay himself), and myself. Graham's attitude was that if the film was about him, then it should address all the aspects of his life, including our relationship. The director and producer wanted to interview me about Graham's work and career, but when I asked how I would be introduced, the film-makers grew bashful and even vague. 'Something like longtime friend,' was one suggestion when I asked how they planned to explain the queer in the 3D Yello T-shirt who would pop up throughout their film talking about Graham. Talking this through with Graham, I planned my own introduction.

At the time, I was music editor (rock, folk, jazz, as was) on *Time Out* magazine, but it seemed dishonest to let this professional tag obscure the true reason I was appearing in the film. So, togged up in jeans and a headache-inducing T-shirt promoting a then little-known Swiss electropop outfit, I met the film crew in the ornamental gardens at Bracknell early in the blazing July afternoon when *Hoarded Dreams* was to be premièred. As the questions proceeded it became apparent that the big issue wasn't going to be brought up, so I waited for the chance and jumped in: 'Well, as a critic and also as Graham's lover …' The film crew twitched perceptibly, but continued regardless. It was over in a few minutes.

Despite the film crew lights which seemed to double the already considerable July heat in the festival tent, and despite the disruption of a crane camera dollying back and forth along a little railway track in front of the stage, *Hoarded Dreams* won a rapturous standing ovation, praise shared jointly by composer and performers. As he had asked, I had a drink ready when Graham came offstage after conducting the band for over an hour. I congratulated him on the piece and kissed him briefly on the lips. When we saw a rough cut of the film, it turned out that the film crew had spotted and filmed this scene from about a hundred yards away. This harmless act of affection made it into the final edit, as part of the closing credits.

When Channel 4 transmitted the documentary that autumn, a columnist in a British jazz magazine took exception to the personal detail in the film, in particular my declaration of my carnal interest in its subject and the closing kiss. The columnist, the aptly christened Jim Godbolt, complained 'although John may be Graham's inamorata', what did that information add to the music? The answer, of course, is absolutely zilch, just as the information that Cathy Berberian and Luciano Berio were married had no great musical significance, although no columnist ever asked them to keep quiet about their relationship. Passing over the feminine noun 'inamorata', which Godbolt probably intended as a sly dig at effeminate homos, Godbolt's complaints, which were discussed at length by friends in the media and music circles, also carried a second-order meaning, the tedious and dubious line beloved of *Telegraph* and *Spectator* columnists, 'I don't mind gays but ...', a form of wish-fulfilment censorship which I consider to be little more than gentrified fascism. The subtext of Godbolt's column – couched in what he clearly hoped was good-natured, lightly-humorous, first-names, don't-get-me-wrong-but language – was an urgent need to erase this evidence that queers may have infiltrated his exclusive train spotters' club. I retaliated by making some childish but perfectly legal abusive remarks about Godbolt in a gossip column I edited on *Time Out*, and left the brouhaha to fade away, unaware that the inamorata imbroglio was already sneaking back up on us. Weirder still, we were both about to undergo the unique experience of being inned – reverse outed, that is, being pushed back into the closet – and at the hands of none other than a lesbian.

In 1990, lesbian photographer Valerie Wilmer published her autobiography, *Mama Said There'd Be Days Like This*. Wilmer's professional pedigree is exceptional; nearly a lifetime of journalism and fine black-and-white photography of jazz musicians, images won by hard work, commitment, devotion and a readiness to make sacrifices on many levels. Wilmer's cred is unassailable, but when she packs her camera away I have to invoke the Orwell/Dali distinction. Our first, and as far as I can recall only, conversation, at a Bracknell jazz festival in the late 1970s, was marked by an extraordinary hostility on Wilmer's part. Knowing that she had produced a number of superb illustrated books about jazz musicians, I asked if she had ever thought of publishing a book about gay jazz musicians. 'He's the only one,' she sneered, gesturing at Graham. Wilmer is friends with virtually every black American jazz musician, and given the foregoing this was either a lie or breath-taking naivety.

Wilmer finally came out in her autobiography, which, while belated, is far more than untold other lesbians and gay men in the music scene have ever done. Discussing homophobia and the jazz scene, she detailed the circumstances of the inamorata imbroglio, *but without ever naming either of the queers involved*. What made this all the more odd was that Wilmer had called Graham to ask if he minded if she used the story in her book. Feeling that the story was as out in the open as it was ever likely to get, he told her to write what she liked. Wilmer had to be aware that Graham was out, and she should at least have been aware that in my journalism (on the AIDS crisis, on gay film and literature, and as a queer pop fan) I was as out as I could possibly be without starting to bore the readers. Wilmer may have been acting out of professional spite – we worked for magazines that were hostile rivals in the same market – but to pursue this antagonism on such a personal level was graceless, petty and mean. The Godbolts of the world will always be with us, the 'why do they have to shove it down people's throats?' brigade, whose seemingly reasonable manner in fact masks an irrational loathing of queers. But to be shoved back in the closet by someone whom you might have marched alongside is something else entirely.

The story of queer jazz does seem to have a happier future, however, and even in the time since I began researching this book the jazz world has been changing for the better. One event worth note and even celebration is the highly public coming out by the vibra-phonist, bandleader and composer Gary Burton. In 1989, Burton, teaching at Berklee in Boston, held a party to which he invited his band, his lover Earl, college staff and friends from Boston's gay scene. In 1993, Burton was the subject of a Public Broadcast System documentary, half of which was devoted to his career and half to his outspoken attitude about his sexuality. The documentary sparked off much media interest, and at the time of writing Burton is still dealing with the (mostly pleasant) knock-on effects of his high-profile coming out.

Burton was, by all accounts, an exceptionally gifted child, who mastered the marimba at six, vibes at ten, and had moved on to the piano in his early teens. While a student at Berklee, Burton began to develop his extraordinary four-mallet technique, which effectively gives him three or four arms and hands to play with. The increased subtlety of technique this produces gives Burton's playing a singing, almost pianistic sound, and is certainly far removed from the style of a traditional vibraphonist like Milt Jackson of the Modern Jazz Quartet.

Burton first came to note when he joined the prestigious George Shearing Quintet, a fairly mainstream band but one which gave Burton the space to shine. He moved on to join Stan Getz's Quartet in 1964, where he worked alongside bassist Steve Swallow, who would become a regular collaborator in years to come. In 1967, composer Carla Bley wrote *A Genuine Tong Funeral*, a 'dark opera without words', for Burton's own quintet and jazz orchestra. His quartet then comprised Burton, Swallow, guitarist Larry Coryell (soon to form the jazz-rock group 11th House) and a drummer who remained anonymous, probably for contractual reasons. As well as giving Burton and band an imaginative and adventurous setting, the work prefigured Bley's own monumental *Escalator over the Hill*. In 1971, Burton recorded his historic collaboration with fellow Berklee graduate Keith Jarrett, a work of joy on which both men excel themselves.

Throughout the 1970s and 1980s, Burton produced a steady stream of albums, duets with Swallow, quartets and quintets featuring the likes of Pat Metheny, Eberhard Weber and Bob Moses, of elegantly ruminative music, mostly for ECM (although recently for his new label, GRP) and for many listeners capturing and even defining the German label's smooth house style. A typical Burton album is the 1976 ECM release, *Passengers*, a particularly beautiful collection of pieces which showcases the dexterity and grace of Burton's playing. He was also one of the core musicians on his friend k.d. lang's platinum-selling *Ingenue* album.

Burton says that he probably knew that he was gay at an early age, 'about the age of thirteen or fourteen. I probably knew even earlier, but was effectively denying it.' He was already embarked on a career trajectory that would take him into the professional music world. He recorded his first professional sessions at the age of seventeen, and went on the road as a working musician at nineteen. 'I was a child entertainer from the age of eight,' he says, 'and I have always suffered from the "goldfish bowl" syndrome of being conscious of people watching and judging me.'

Burton was able, he says, to have good, loving and supportive relationships with the opposite sex, and is still good friends with his second wife and the two children, now in their teens, they had. But throughout thirty years of marriages and long-term relationships, he was also aware of his attraction to other men, and at times pursued gay encounters and even relationships between heterosexual relationships. Although he was, he says, perfectly happy with his sexual orientation, in the early years of his career, 'It just wasn't something that I could risk confronting, given my developing career and visibility, and the tenor of the times growing up in the fifties and sixties.'

The jazz world he entered in the early 1960s was, he says, 'macho in the extreme'. No one was writing frank biographies of Bessie Smith then, still less discussing the private life of someone like Billy Strayhorn. 'I have always thought that if I were in a different field,' he says, 'either one which didn't involve notoriety (like jazz), or one such as classical music, where gay musicians were more visible and available as role models, I would have felt comfortable "being myself" fairly early on.' He adds, however, that his reluctance to come out had nothing whatsoever to do with 'fear of parental scorn or moral or religious views'. 'It was career-based,' he says, 'absolutely. I had a wonderful thing going and it was far more important to continue with my music than anything else. I was quite willing to sacrifice my peace of mind to a considerable extent.'

It was only when Burton felt he had achieved most of what he felt he could achieve, had established a reputation as a world-class virtuoso of his instrument, and began to put less store in the opinions of others, that he could approach his own homosexuality. 'I finally reached a point where two things converged,' he says. 'I was getting older, and less concerned about proving myself, and less worried about what people thought. I wanted to live what was left of my life without having to look over my shoulder. At the same time, the attitudes toward being gay were much more tolerant and accepting, in the eighties and nineties especially.'

Six years ago, prompted by an encounter with a gay man whom Burton found very attractive, he decided that the time was right to come out. 'I'll never forget that experience of freedom, after thirty-five years of keeping it hidden, always having monitored everything I said or did, so as not to give myself away.'

These are familiar feelings for anyone who has ever come out, and as for Burton 'giving himself away', he found to his surprise that two members of his own band had already presumed that he was gay. Indeed, Burton says that both of his wives were aware that there was a gay side to his personality, and that he had had gay relationships before and inbetween both marriages. He adds that his sexuality was not the reason that these relationships ended.

He believes that 'of all the forms of music, jazz is the least tolerant of homosexuality'. Over the years he has been aware of a small number of gay jazz musicians, 'including a few who achieved a high degree of fame', although none, as far as he is aware, have ever gone public with their sexuality. 'I can understand why a bandleader in the early years could not dare consider such a thing,' he says, 'but it's hard for me to understand it remaining so in the current times.' He feels, however, that 'jazz's public image does not fit well with being a gay person'. Stereotypes, to which both straight and gay people subscribe, make it difficult for a homosexual to be accepted as a jazz musician, although not, of course, impossible. 'There is this clear perception of masculinity and macho characteristics in jazz,' he says. 'We want our musicians to kick ass. These are still the terms in common use. There's a kind of athletic implication, too. Playing the long solo, working it out, building and building. The inference is also kind of sexual. Jazz, rock'n'roll, all present very strong sexual imagery.'

'Unfortunately (or not),' he adds, 'a lot of jazz's present is closely tied up with its history. Old imagery will not die quickly or without a fight. Many people still persist in wanting jazz to be played by fucked-up addicts and alcoholics, in cramped smoky clubs, while wearing garish clothes and silly little hats and sunglasses, talking in jive-talk. I get complaints all the time about not looking the part, and about jazz not being the same in a concert hall.' He agrees that there is a hidden history of homosexuality in jazz, although we might equally call it a history of homosexuality being hidden in jazz. 'It's not like there was a conspiracy or anything, at least no one ever approached me with an admonishment to do the right thing for the art and keep my inclinations secret. It was just no more welcome in jazz than it was in national sports, or various other professions.' He says that it's a shame that we do not know about all the lesbians and gays who have worked in the jazz field, adding 'We're all the worse off because of the closeted lives through the decades. The historians have absolutely avoided the issue, of course. They're all suck-ups to the history of the art, and don't want to raise issues that might, in their eyes, denigrate the art form. Too bad. It makes them lousy historians. But, then, jazz historians have never been interested in the facts. They've always been more interested in the myths. It's the myths that have drawn them to it to begin with, rather than true intellectual curiosity. How can someone in love with something be truly objective?'

Unusually, Burton says that he experienced two different responses when he started to come out. Where he may have feared resistance or hostility, he said that band members, musician friends, and staff and authorities at Berklee were 'totally supportive, with even the college president bringing up the subject to reassure me that my partner and I were absolutely welcome and respected'. He believed that audiences 'if they identified me as a "queen", would judge my work in the context of their prejudices and stereotypes', although this has not happened so far. He had also feared that some friends and acquaintances might not want to work with him after he came out as gay. Again, many of his friends and acquaintances 'went out of their way' to voice their support for him. 'Either this is indicative of greater enlightenment among musicians than I had expected,' he says, 'or I have very good taste in friends.'

While he says, a number of times, that the jazz scene is still perceived, erroneously I feel, as macho, it should also be recognized that this is a new generation of musicians, and listeners. Burton's generation demonstrated against, and many even fought in, Vietnam. It lived through the civil rights campaigns of the 1960s, through Woodstock and Altamont, through women's liberation and gay liberation. It would be impossible to live through this and retain intact the attitudes that Gary Burton encountered when he entered the music industry in the late 1950s. Given the vaguely defined social profile of the average jazz fan – they tend towards the middle-class, university-educated, liberal, leftish, at least in Britain and, I'd say, urban America – they must surely be among the people who have created a climate that makes it easier to be out as gay today. If, as I suspect, they have gay friends, then why shouldn't they also have out gay jazz musicians in their record collections?

Perhaps the most unusual of all, however, was the reaction Gary Burton encountered from the gay community, in his home town of Boston, and in other American cities. On a personal level, Burton found the experience of coming out as a gay man in modern America a quite wondrous experience. Coming out as a gay jazz musician was a different matter. 'I discovered early on,' he says, 'that the gay community as a whole is practically anti-jazz, and at the very least is indifferent to it.'

He says that, when he came out and started meeting other gay men, he began to conduct a straw poll of their musical tastes. The answers he got were along the lines of 'Show music, disco, opera, classical, k.d. lang, Judy Garland, etc.' I'd be tempted to suggest he was trying the wrong sort of bars, and almost certainly the wrong sort of queers, but this would be to denigrate the experience of many people who enjoy this music. It is almost certainly down to an accident of experience that Gary Burton hasn't met the sort of queers I've met who love anything from Ellington to Braxton, like the chair of an AIDS charity whom I once found whistling – without a hint of irony – Thelonious Monk's 'Straight No Chaser' while he worked on the charity's switchboard.

Gary Burton's experience was to be repeated as he explored the local and national gay community. He tried to interest a local gay bookstore, which also stocks records, in stocking his records, but the store ultimately declined, 'because jazz just didn't fit in with their concept'. He advertised his concerts in regional gay publications, but to little or no avail. He approached a 'national gay magazine' with the idea of their running a profile on an out gay jazz musician (him). The magazine's response was, 'Jazz? Why would anyone be interested in reading about that?' He finds himself confronting the 'great irony' of being 'a gay person in a field of music seen as macho, and I'm a jazz musician in a gay community which isn't interested'.

He says that he has now come to the conclusion that there are basically two ways to approach one's sexuality in any of the professional fields that place one in the public eye. 'Some individuals include their gay identity as part of their public persona, and it becomes a very colourful aspect of the expression they convey to their audience. My friend k.d. lang comes to mind as a perfect example. A wonderful musician and singer, but also clearly expressing her gay identity in everything she does and says, and it holds her audience all the more enthralled.'

Then there are those, and Burton probably includes himself in their ranks, 'for whom it is not natural to include their gay identity in their public image'. He believes that the same is true of heterosexual performers; that there are some who quite naturally include their sexuality in their public persona, while others do not. Burton feels that he is a performer whose sexuality is not wholly relevant to his work. 'I'm out to anyone and everyone,' he says. 'I don't announce it from the stage as I start the concerts, but I make no attempt to hide it, either. It's just not all that relevant to my performing.'

Burton's experience throws up a number of interesting topics, not least the notion that some arts are perceived as queer-friendly, while others are perceived as queer-unfriendly. The friendly ones tend to be those associated with a certain lifestyle, a certain nightlife. That they should also be the ones sanctioned by gay magazines should come as no surprise; much gay publishing is simply an excuse to print highly lucrative ads, and content merely reflects a received notion of a stereotypical gay readership profile. Gay jazz fans, like gay Grateful Dead fans (yes, I've met them), just have to look elsewhere for media support of their interests.

The queer-unfriendly arts tend towards the abstract: jazz, avant-garde music, contemporary art, modernist literature, performance art, experimental film. Yet all of these, barring jazz, receive occasional coverage in the gay media. Contemplating this, for a while I wondered if the difference was between gay-themed art and non-gay-themed art, but that distinction breaks down under its own weight too. It could be accessibility – I've not met that many gay men at concerts of avant-garde music, either – but equally it could be the perception of the audience. If a large audience doesn't exist for jazz per se, why should a large audience of gay listeners exist for gay jazz? It is true that education and the pressures of commerce – in clubs and venues, on radio and television, in newspapers and magazines – get in the way of a potential audience. Few people are going to buy tickets for a concert if popular opinion tells them they are going to hear one long and noisy car crash.

While all this has disappointed Gary Burton, he can still say, 'Whatever, I'm a happy man these days. I finally was able to come to terms with my identity and it has made me a better musician, and a more confident and productive person, and I look forward to every day of my life now ... I've gotten to eat my cake and have it, too. I have had the career I always wanted, and although belatedly, I've been able to come out, and be myself, too. There was a time when having both probably wouldn't have been possible. Now, I just feel the need to hurry and catch up with all the things I missed out on because I was hiding from it all these years.'

And even though he still says, rather ruefully, 'I have found only a handful of gays who actually follow jazz,' that's still a handful more than Armistead Maupin knows.

Chapter eight

Exhuming Elvis

AS we approach the shallows of recent popular musical history, we should bear two things in mind. In the case of the blues, jazz and songs from shows, music hall and radio, popular music had always been racially segregated, with black musicians producing their own music, and whites theirs, for two separate audiences, with the former often originating music which was then appropriated by the latter. In the birth of rock'n'roll, black and white music converged. Some musics are still predominantly associated with racial background; soul and funk are considered, at their most 'authentic' best, to be black musics, and the various forms of guitar rock, from heavy metal to speed/thrash/death metal, are, even though rooted in black music, essentially white. But the strict divisions between white and black music, and white and black musicians and bands (and their audiences), began to disappear in the 1950s.

Secondly, rock'n'roll was born during – and perhaps because of – a postwar boom that saw the birth of the teenager and a move towards general (if slow-moving) social emancipation. This was a form of music wholly different from previous ones in the ways it was made, the ways it was distributed and promoted, and the ways it was consumed. For all the youthful rebelliousness of some of its main exponents, it was also very much a commodity, needing marketing and promotion, and requiring sophisticated publicity and image-making. Where earlier forms of popular music had simply relied on the music to promote itself, or had invented a simplistic gimmick like an outfit or name, or had relied on natural good looks or Hollywood notions of glamour, rock'n'roll required niche marketing within a volatile market whose tastes and ideas of what was good at the time and what was not – a sound, a look, an attitude, a mode of dress – was in a constant state of flux. More important to our considerations was the fact that personality, image, background and private life became important in a performer's career. While it was initially nurtured by independent record labels, rock'n'roll quickly became big business, in America and then in Britain. Writer and broadcaster Charlie Gillett records, in his excellent history of rock, *The Sound of the City*, that within a matter of years after its birth, the American rock'n'roll scene was dominated by five major record labels, who controlled the vast majority of releases. Where blues and jazz musicians were at liberty to conduct scandalous lifestyles without risking their careers, rock'n'roll, again despite its rebellious image, was tied to a publicity machine modelled on Hollywood. Like that propaganda operation, the rock'n'roll publicists cleaved to Hollywood's moral code, even when their charges did not. Where many Hollywood stars spent their lives in what Vito Russo called the celluloid closet, so many pop stars spent theirs in what writer Boze Hadleigh called, rather predictably, the vinyl closet.

It is also fair to say that, in the rush to get rock'n'roll out into the market place, what embryonic or underground queer sensibilities may have existed at the time would have been swept aside in the stampede. Whatever revolutionary gloss hindsight may lay on rock'n'roll, this was the 1950s, when most teenagers of school age were in bed by nine. It is true that rock'n'roll delineated a *langue d'amour* for the emergent teenager, but in reality this was only giving a name to a new morality that had probably sprung up during the war. Rock'n'roll may have been pushing at the barriers of conventional morality – the name itself derives from another black slang word for fucking, and most pop songs were slyly encoded tales of proposal, longing and desire – but mostly it reflected the moral consensus, certainly as far as deviant sex was concerned. Teenagers at the time, and their historians ever since, may have felt they were changing the world, but the stories rock'n'roll told had been around since Chaucer and Boccaccio.

What *was* new was the commodification of these things, and the rush to exploit the market in the fetish object, the record. Charlie Gillett reports, among other things, that the industry – labels and radio stations – kept a tight control on the number of 'wild' rock'n'roll records that were given exposure. He further reports that most industry pundits thought that rock'n'roll was a passing phase that would burn itself out in a year or so.

Of the five strands of rock'n'roll that Gillett identifies in the early 1950s – northern band rock'n'roll, New Orleans dance blues, Memphis country rock, Chicago rhythm and blues, and vocal group rock'n'roll – only two might be even vaguely linked to a queer sensibility. New Orleans dance blues mutated out of the bars and brothels of the city's notorious Storyville area, where 'dirty' and queer blues would have been commonplace. (New Orleans also has a long and continuing tradition of tolerating queer culture, at least in certain sections of the French Quarter.) Memphis country rock, and its near neighbour western swing, grew up out of the country tradition, and, despite its vigorously heterosexual image today, it is rooted in the same-sex culture of the prairies. The homoerotic subtext of this community remains largely unexcavated, but in his *Gay American History*, historian Jonathan Ned Katz records two visual examples of the dances that were common in this all-male environment. One, an illustration from the 1890s, resembles a Tom of Finland party scene where the proportions have been reduced to a realistic representation of men dancing together. The other, an undated photograph, features two boys, one a teenager and the other a pre-teen, attempting what looks like a waltz, while next to them two men in hats and cowboy boots dance cheek-to-cheek. (Armistead Maupin once told me, only partly in jest, that such cowboy dances were where the hankie code – for leader and led – may have originated. Certainly, the tradition lives on, if only in an act of bizarre mimesis, in the line dances and waltzes of America's gay western bars.)

Neither New Orleans dance blues nor Memphis country rock, however, bequeathed much of a queer sensibility to rock'n'roll. In fact, they grew up together. According to Charlie Gillett, the word 'rock' had been around in song titles as early as 1948, the year Henry Hay, founder of America's Mattachine Society, thought up the idea of a 'homophile' support group. By 1951, when the Mattachine Society was established (Mattachine, Hay told Jonathan Ned Katz, came from a French quasi-mystic group active in the Middle Ages), the first straightahead rock record, Gunter Lee Carr's 'We're Gonna Rock', was released. The following year, legendary American DJ Alan Freed appropriated the term rock'n'roll for the hot (and largely black) music he was playing on his New York radio show, and the year after that rock'n'roll crashed into the mainstream with Bill Haley and the Comets' 'Rock Around the Clock'.

These were not happy times in which to be queer. As the McCarthy anti-communist witchhunts worked through an A-to-Z of Hollywood's great and good in the House UnAmerican Activities Committee, the American right was trawling for the queer menace, too. There was a highly publicized purge of homosexuals from the State Department, and police agents provocateurs were active in gay cruising areas (a founding member of Mattachine was arrested by one, and one of the Society's first campaigns was to prove his innocence). With war in Korea unfolding and the Cold War at its height, homosexual rights went largely undefended in one of the darker moments of American history, and this was echoed in anti-gay campaigns in Britain (such as the questionings and arrests that saw Benjamin Britten interviewed, for example).

It is little surprise, then, that rock'n'roll was essentially het-erosexual in its subject matter, even if some of its performers (Little Richard, Johnnie Ray) weren't heterosexual themselves. As a small controlled teen explosion, rock'n'roll had to work out its own obsessions with boy meets girl before it could begin even to contem-plate the possibility of boy meets boy or girl meets girl. Semiologists have decoded the 'ooh's, 'yeah's and 'baby's of rock'n'roll and pop, and the references to boys and to girls, to produce encyclopedic breakdowns of pop's romantic signage, but beyond certain code words and furtive simile, pop's *langue d'amour* remained resolutely fey and coy even about respectable heterosexual dalliances. It takes a sharp mind like Gillett's to decode the Everly Brothers' 'All I Have to Do Is Dream', for example, as the nearest rock'n'roll ever got to alluding to masturbation.

Even Little Richard, one of the most flamboyant figures in the history of popular music, and a seminal influence on the form, was reduced to gibberish and code words on his famous 'Rip It Up' (with its references to balling) and 'Tutti Frutti', unless we are to take his historic declamation 'Awopbopaloobop' as onomatapoeia. Initially a gospel singer, who had worked with touring rhythm and blues and gospel revues, Richard scored a hit in 1955 with 'Tutti Frutti', and followed that with a string of other hits, among them the frenzied 'Good Golly Miss Molly', 'Long Tall Sally' and 'Keep A-Knockin''. However, he turned (back) to fundamentalist Christianity in 1957, resisting the lure to record any more of these outrageous and sexually charged tunes and turning back instead to gospel. In 1963 he returned to recording rock'n'roll tunes but Richard never repeated the success of those initial 1950s hits. Nevertheless they assured him a place in the pantheon of rock history, not to mention the numerous rock'n'roll revivals in the intervening years and Richard's own various comebacks. In his autobiography, Richard made much of his early homosexual experiences, and of his subsequent 'conversion' to Christianity and heterosexuality, although at the time he kept this secret, presenting a public image that was more in keeping with the risqué blues tradition of a performer like Fats Waller.

Johnnie Ray, who scored massive chart success on both sides of the Atlantic in 1951 and 1952 with 'Cry' and 'The Little White Cloud That Cried', was not as secretive about his sexuality as Richard, and indeed was arrested on an indecency or 'morals' charge in the 1960s. The critics railed against Ray's extraordinary stage performance, in which his overwrought singing (an effect exacerbated by a congenital hearing defect) broke down into sobs, gasps and tears that could actually send him, quickly dubbed the Nabob of Sob by the media, stumbling from the mike stand. Appearing to go completely to pieces on stage, Ray provoked some of the earliest instances of fan hysteria, at concerts and at public appearances. Contemporary photographs of Ray performing actually bear an uncanny resemblance to Joy Division singer Ian Curtis. The crowd hysterics may seem ironical given Ray's (at the time, hidden) sexuality, but as would be the case with later stars, be it the Beatles or Boy George, mass hysterics by young women did and does not simply equate with desire for the performer in question. It is a form of catharsis, and bonding, in which the individual fan's feelings towards a star can take a variety of forms, from a desire for companionship to a sadistic urge to control.

If rock'n'roll was essentially heterosexual in the 1950s, this is because the new form was still finding its language, and both performers and consumers were negotiating the experiences that it helped them name and discuss. Topics that were taboo in the mainstream were just as taboo in pop. It should also be noted that, while rock'n'roll was delineating teen mating rituals in the ever-shifting argot of the period, this music was being archived and chronicled by, again, heterosexual males with little or no interest in or even awareness of an alternative viewpoint. It was during this period that rock'n'roll acquired its reputation as a rampantly macho and masculinist art form, a living – nay, throbbing – embodiment of every Freudian cliché you care to mention. The tabernacle of this orgiastic new religion was sited in the pelvic cavity of Elvis Aaron Presley, a sacred place revered by the millions who visited it on TV. In his ascendancy as much as his decline into grotesque eating disorders, drug abuse and dementia, Elvis Presley was perceived as the ultimate godlike heterosexual male – well, according to the heterosexual males who wrote the articles and books that said he was. That wasn't necessarily the case if you were, say, a lesbian.

I owe this insight to the lesbian feminist critic Sue Wise, whose 'Sexing Elvis', anthologized in Simon Frith and Andrew Godwin's *On Record* (Routledge), is probably the most exciting single piece of music journalism I have ever read. In fewer than eight succinct pages, Wise manages to undermine nearly half a century of rock criticism, and certainly says more about Elvis Presley than all 232 pages of Greil Marcus's *Dead Elvis*. The beauty of Wise's piece is that in reclaiming her version of Elvis Presley it outlines a near-perfect death-of-the-author theory for pop. In Roland Barthes's original theory, the 'death' of the author elects each new reader as author, as each new reader effectively invents the text anew. In reconsidering her relationship to the Elvis she admired as a teenager, in the light of the feminist and lesbian theories she subscribed to when she came out in her twenties, Wise declares a post-modern open season on Marcus's dead Elvis.

Before doing so, however, Wise has a few bones to pick with virtually all pop historians. Elvis as he is written by heterosexual male critics is, essentially, a fondly remembered hard-on. If adjectives around motion were ascribed to him, they were violent, invasive, penetrative. If animal similes were applied to him, they were always powerful male animals, and powerful male animals that were historically vulnerable to emasculation. If cultural values were pinned to him, they were as a force of revolution, war, insurrection, the overthrow of an existing order. If sexual functions were teased out of his persona, Elvis was King Kong, Errol Flynn, Valentino, Gable and Cagney rolled into one, a distillation of every American male sexual icon boiled down and imprinted on to ten hot inches of hard and horny petroleum by-product. Moreover, Elvis was what all women wanted (if, alas, rarely acquired), and was there to tell women to be good – don't be cruel! – to men.

Well, that's one way of reading it, although it looks a little odd when you consider that his very first hit, 'Heartbreak Hotel', in 1956, was an extraordinarily depressing blues ballad based on the real-life story of a man who checked into a motel to kill himself and left a suicide note saying that he felt so lonely he wanted to die. Some party animal, that Elvis!

Reading Sue Wise, readers can find themselves (at least, this one did) totting up the other Elvis tunes that also do not accord with the image of Presley as a snorting and stamping sex beast. 'Love Me Tender' comes to mind first, possibly the most achingly poignant song about romantic longing in the history of pop, then 'Are You Lonesome Tonight?' followed by 'Can't Help Falling in Love', 'Wooden Heart' (during which the panting fuck god starts singing in *German*, for Chrissakes), 'In the Ghetto', and others, none of which bears the slightest resemblance to the sort of material this mythic Elvis ought to have produced. (In fact, the sort of material this mythic Elvis ought to have produced probably came only a few decades later, with the advent of SM/avant-garde/noise bands like Swans, in particular their 'Raping a Slave' EP.) These Elvis ballads have to be balanced against tougher material like 'Jailhouse Rock' and 'Hound Dog', of course, but even then this doesn't equal out to the work of the man who created the sweatily masculinist and phallocentric edifice of rock'n'roll as it is celebrated before untold teenage males' bedroom mirrors.

Then you think about the Presley sign: the gyroscopic hips,

those heroically askew legs, the arms thrown high (almost as though in surrender). American TV channels at the time focused on the hips, or rather they didn't; they ruled that Presley could only be filmed from the waist up. Rock historians followed the same line. Presley's hips became the ark in which the masculinity of future generations sailed. But take another look at those arms. Doesn't he look a little too vulnerable? Doesn't he, in fact, look a little too willingly vulnerable? *Did Elvis Presley want to be tied up?*

A generous queer reading of Elvis Presley's sexuality would be that, whatever sort of slob and monster he would turn into in later years, the Presley sign signified and celebrated sexual freedom, release, pleasure in the body. This wild and unchannelled energy was written into a heterosexual missionary position by heterosexual men with a vested interest in promoting that activity. This is not to say that Presley was a sexual radical – he called his elders sir and ma'am, joined the army, married young and later became a deranged and paranoid fascist – but that the rebellious sexuality he represented was promptly reined into line with the prevailing values of the 1950s.

There are a further few crimps in the masculinist view of Presley the rock icon. Compared to other rock'n'rollers – Chuck Berry, Bo Diddley and T-Bone Walker, the man responsible for the idea of the guitar as phallic stage prop (Gillett) – Presley's stage performance was actually rather subdued. This might in part be explained away by the tendency of white musicians to appropriate and bowdlerize raunchy black material for consumption by white audiences, and it probably had a lot to do with the image manipulation by his legendary manager, 'Colonel' Tom Parker. Yet the rock historians, who normally disparage populist incarnations of a style when there are rootsier, 'authentic' and ego-enhancingly obscure versions of that style to which they can fashionably subscribe, have, by and large, gone with Presley, where a purist might have gone with T-Bone Walker or Berry. This may have something to do with the childhood experiences of rock historians in general, and it might also have something to do with unthinking institutionalized racism. Certainly, it seems to go entirely against the grain of heterosexual rock mythology by ignoring a whole raft of second-order clichés about black sexuality.

There is still a further wrinkle here. In representing Presley as a rock Thor bestriding the world of the 1950s teenager, the masculinist vision of rock history seems to imply that women had somehow been waiting for this deity to arrive – and, moreover, that they knew exactly what to do with this deity when it did arrive. Previously chaste young women in bobby sox and three-quarter length petticoated frocks who had dreamed of holding hands with some cheesy prefabricated crooner pin-up were, it seemed, transformed overnight into wild and insatiable sluts who just wanted to get their legs round those hips.

Or did they? Like Johnnie Ray, Presley certainly provoked wild and often hysterical reactions from crowds of young women, but the nature of those reactions has always, *always*, been decoded by heterosexual men, not just rock critics but national media drones whose job it has always been to present these phenomena in ways their proprietors would like them to be seen. And it is in the very nature of journalism to inflate such phenomena in ways that will sell newspapers. Not only did this interpretation of events fit snugly into the social order of the period, it had the additional bonus of reassuring and reaffirming the masculinity of the males who were mediating this information for popular consumption. What none of them had reckoned on, of course, was that there were probably quite a few future dykes in Elvis's audience, women who, moreover, did not consume the cultural product 'Elvis Presley' as men thought they did.

In fact, it is quite likely that Sue Wise liked Elvis for the reasons that most pop fans, female or male, like the pop stars they do; because the star's work sounds a resonance with their own feelings, that they feel an affinity with the star, accepting the work as seeming autobiography but admitting, also, that the pop song is a work of fiction and play, and that as music with certain emotions spelled out in it, it serves a need, a desire, or supplies pleasure. Sue Wise sets out two Elvises, the Wagnerian hunk and the guy in touch with his *tendresse*, and decides that the difference between the two is defined solely by the heterosexual male constructions of the Elvis icon.

Almost certainly, the Elvis she communed with in the privacy of her shared bedroom as a young girl was the latter, and I believe that will have been the case with the majority of his fans, including some of the men. Because it has to be acknowledged that the sensitive side of Elvis could have taught some men (like an Elvis-mad older brother of mine) how to name and negotiate their own emotions. We also have to consider the likelihood, given the era, given the country, and given the political climate, that in its time Elvis's work itself could have been read as queer. (There is also the small matter that much of the male journalism that built the Presley edifice is itself freighted with a homoerotic subtext. Most, however, don't seem to know where admiration ends and desire begins.)

Following Sue Wise's line of thought, you soon arrive at the suspicion that most rock historians probably had at least one hand in their pocket playing with their marbles while they wrote. There is also the spooky possibility that, in the manner of an episode of *The Twilight Zone*, rock history may one day prove to have been written by a single, spotty, twenty-one-year-old Led Zeppelin fan with a hang-up about the size of his penis.

For the meantime, we should marvel at the achievement of one lesbian, and apply such readings to the rest of rock history. If a lone dyke can bring this monstrous fiction crashing to earth, who knows what an army of lovers might do.

Chapter nine

Girls Together Outrageously

THE history of women's involvement in the music industry, on either side of the glass window of the studio control room, and on either side of the executive desk, might be summed up by the attitude evident in one well-known sentence.

There are groups, and then there are girl groups.

Even when women overcame upbringing and gained access to music education, economic independence and the self-empowerment to make, produce, engineer or manage music, they still had to contend with the male playground of the music industry and the male club of the electronic and print media which promoted and controlled the music.

There are always exceptions: Motown superbassist Carole Kaye, who must be heartily sick of being wheeled out as an early example of Women In Rock, and Brill building composers such as Carole King and Ellie Greenwich, who still had to contend with the fact that they sometimes lost composing credits because they were women. Some of the earliest rock'n'roll composers were women, and in the 1960s some women performers, Lulu and Sandie Shaw, for example, were managed by women. Women had also, of course, long been very welcome in the form of all-girl harmony groups, black or white, although we have only to contemplate the careers of women controlled by the likes of Phil Spector and Ike Turner to realize the disadvantages there. Black women blues and jazz singers could be said to have enjoyed a greater degree of autonomy than women working in rock'n'roll and pop, but that was often at the expense of commercial success.

It took the advent of the 1960s for women performers to be offered or to develop alternatives themselves to the either/or choice of sweet/vulnerable roles they had been given to play in the past. Even these were shackled to the ideologies of the times, be they Beat Girls like Sandie Shaw, Kathy Kirby or Dusty Springfield, or the later school of confessional singer-songwriters, such as Dory Previn and Joni Mitchell, who sang of themselves in terms of their relationships with (normally more powerful) men. There was and remains an honourable tradition of independent and self-assertive women working in the field of folk (discussed at length later in this book), notably with such figures as Joan Baez and Ronnie Gilbert of the Weavers, and the folk and acoustic music scene still acts as a launching pad for original and self-defining women performers, although through the decades it has evolved as a parallel industry to the popular mainstream.

It would take further decades before women would break free of male-defined categories (and it would take until 1982 before an all-women band, The Go-Gos, would reach number one in the American album charts), but there is also a secret history at work here which, while much of it remains secret, and will probably do so until some unlikely radical change overtakes Western society, should not be allowed to go forgotten or ignored.

There is a feminist, and a lesbian, subtext to the history of pop, although it is covert rather than overt, and the passage of time tends to diminish its power and effect. If the pop industry wasn't going to stand for independent and assertive heterosexual women, it most certainly wasn't going to stand for dykes on mikes. Rumour of lesbianism has attached itself to a number of women singers from the 1960s, although none of them has felt able to go public with this information. Some have even managed to collaborate with biographers and keep this information secret. This isn't a very happy state of affairs for any of the individuals involved, but the pressures on lesbian performers in the mainstream are immense, and immensely greater than the pressures on, for example, gay men in a similarly closeted position.

In nearly two decades of peripheral involvement with the music industry, the number of lesbians I have met in the music industry can still be counted on the fingers of one hand. One, a record plugger who was aware that I was an out gay journalist, came out to me over lunch, but pleaded with me to keep her secret for her (which of course I did). She wanted to come out, but felt that the situation at work would become impossible, not surprisingly considering the number of heterosexual pinheads at large in the music industry. Another had simply spot-welded herself into her closet and would probably never come out. It took the advent of punk, and the arrival of the Naylor sisters, Liz and Pat, as press workers at Rough Trade records, the first two out lesbians I met in the industry, for the music industry to acquire its first out dykes. They both move across the dividing line between media and labels, writing for papers, and becoming involved in indie labels like One Little Indian. Liz was also involved in the British branch of Riot Grrrl, managing leading RG band Huggy Bear, and is nowadays at the centre of Queercore, running Catcall Records. But there has been no noticeable sea-change in the homophobic attitudes of the music industry in general.

Given this lamentable situation, we have to be especially careful when contemplating the history of lesbians in pop, a story written in disappearing ink. Apart from those singers who are dogged with rumours of a secret lesbian lifestyle, we might consider the 1960s a dyke-free zone, until Gillian G. Gaar, in her exhaustive history of women in rock, *She's a Rebel*, reveals that Carol McDonald, of Goldie and the Gingerbreads, was a lesbian who felt she could not come out (although she did with her next band, Isis). Similarly, we should be careful when considering the earliest Women In Rock, bands like Pamela Des Barres' GTOs (Girls Together Outrageously), Bertha, or Fanny. Fanny, the most successful of these pioneering women's hard rock groups, may have learned their licks and their moves from the boys (we are, after all, talking about the very early 1970s here) but they grew on into the feminist and women's music movement. Bassist June Millington, who with guitarist sister Jean was the frontline of Fanny, later became a respected producer for Cris Williamson, among others, and, in the preferred terminology, is out as a woman-identified woman. While McDonald and Millington are only two examples of lesbians working in pop, you can take it as read that they are only the tip of the iceberg. Lesley Gore recently appeared as a 'gay icon' on the cover of the *Village Voice*, and Marianne Faithfull's autobiography, *Faithfull*, details her lesbian affairs.

While most – almost all – lesbians were forced by circumstance to hide their sexuality, one, just one, was so out, so far out, that she puts every other lesbian performer, even k.d. lang, in the shade. Indeed, it seems strange that no others followed her outrageous, in-your-face example. Janis Joplin was queer as fuck a quarter of a century before either the term or the political statement became fashionable, before either might have even been contemplated.

In the easygoing 1960s, Joplin slept with both sexes, and shuffled partners as her passions and circumstances dictated, but her major relationships were with women. She pursued sex with men, usually younger men, sometimes fellow junkies, but this would seem to have been in search of a form of approval, or reciprocated desire. Her most rewarding relationships appear to have been with other dykes.

More books have been written about Joplin than Joplin released albums, and only half of the official albums (excluding hits compilations and cobbled-together out-take 'rareties') were actually released while Joplin was alive. She released *Cheap Thrills*, with Big Brother and the Holding Company, in 1968, and *I Got Dem Ol' Kozmic Blues Again Mama* the following year with the Kozmic Blues Band. She was dead of a heroin overdose before her third album, *Pearl* (containing her only American number one single, Kris Kristofferson's 'Me and Bobby McGee') was released in 1971.

Writers often mention her admiration of Odetta, Bessie Smith, Billie Holiday and Leadbelly, and contemporaries such as Otis Redding, in a talismanic manner, as though the 'authentic' black blues sound might rub off on Joplin's voice. She sounds like none of these artists. Her voice was/is her own, white, a little thin, and with a country twang at the back, but Joplin was capable of an intensity that could flood the listener's veins with ice. Her performance at the 1967 Monterey Pop Festival, caught in edited form in the film *Monterey Pop*, captures Joplin in flight with two of her set classics, 'Try' and Willie Mae Thornton's 'Ball and Chain'. The musical highlight of the film, Joplin produces heart-stopping tension with her convulsive, foot-stamping performance. The Who had to resort to their trademark vandalism, and Jimi Hendrix to oral sex and arson on his own guitar, even to approach a similar level of intensity.

There are also more Janis Joplins than there are albums by the real Joplin, one for each of the books that friends, lovers, her sister Laura and sundry strangers produced. While certain facts and events – gigs, sessions, seductions, fights, other people's overdoses, trips of a variety of kinds – recur as furniture in each book, characters are shifted up and down the cast list in such a violent manner that some events are unrecognizable from book to book. Her sister Laura's memoir can, at least, be regarded as a heartfelt effort to record her sister's life in as dignified manner as possible (given the circumstances). Others, however, made themselves the focus of the Joplin story (Peggy Caserta, *Going Down with Janis*) or felt they were in direct competition with the authors of other biographies of Joplin and had to put a different spin on previously available material (Ellis Amburn's *Pearl*). Some figures are left anonymous in one volume and named in another; others given prominence in one but upstaged in another. At one memorable juncture, Ellis Amburn tries to set two authors, Caserta and Myra Friedman, against each other, but ends up undermining his own authority.

With the exception of sister Laura, who may have her own reasons for not being entirely honest about her sister's often sleazoid life, none of these people is to be trusted. It takes a complete outsider, Bessie Smith biographer Chris Albertson, to give the true story of Joplin's involvement in the campaign to buy a headstone for Smith's grave years after she was buried and the money for the stone was stolen by her husband Jack Gee. After a Philadelphia woman started the campaign in a regional newspaper, Joplin paid half the money for the stone, but stayed away from the dedication ceremony, fearing, according to Albertson, that her attendance might turn the event into a rock star photo opportunity. Peggy Caserta, who paints herself as Joplin's career-long soul mate in *Going Down with Janis*, ignores this, possibly one of the most endearing stories that survives about Joplin, entirely, and Amburn merely notes inaccurately that Joplin 'paid for' the headstone. It is, in fact, one of the most dignified and touching stories from a life wedded to controversy. Similarly, it takes another outsider, Gillian G. Gaar, to suggest that, rather than falling victim to her own gargantuan appetites, Joplin was probably the victim of a wider and larger problem – sexism, homophobia, right-wing politics, the male fear of unconventional women – which generated those self-destructive habits in the first place.

There can be little doubt, however, that whatever the number of lovers, frequency of orgasms, the male–female ratio of lovers or the value Joplin invested in her relations with either sex (and even prurient hetero Ellis Amburn errs on the side of her fundamental lesbian emotions), Janis Joplin was a woman who had a healthy relationship with her libido. Moreover, she acted on it in what appears to have been an uninhibited and outspoken manner. While free love may have been a hippie tenet of her era, it still does not explain the Joplin phenomenon in full.

Depending on which biography you read, Joplin was either a despised Carrie-like figure at school or a highly popular and rather unconventional student. Both stories converge in her late 1950s teens, when Joplin, beset by weight and complexion problems, transformed herself into a beatnik. Peggy Caserta claims that Joplin told her she dropped out into the beat scene, taking casual, low-pay jobs and straying into the folk and blues scene. Ellis Amburn describes her as a talented and promising art student, a voracious reader (Kerouac, Gurdjieff, Owen, Fitzgerald, Hardy, Wolfe) and a sparky and inquisitive intellectual who discovered her blues talent by accident.

Both stories have her departing her hated home town of Port Arthur, Texas, with the assistance of a boyfriend, and eventually finding herself in San Francisco. Peggy Caserta's Janis tells Peggy, some way into their own full-tilt boogie relationship, that she had had another woman partner in the past. Ellis Amburn's Janis falls in with the beat dyke rat pack in the bars up in North Beach, plunging headlong into the speed subculture and generally behaving like a babehound.

Whatever value-system each writer subscribes to – and you get a very real sense that scores are being settled in the way certain people are featured in these books – most seem to agree that Joplin was lured into singing by a friend who knew that the San Francisco band Big Brother and the Holding Company were looking for a singer. In fact, some of them had heard Joplin singing at an open-mike night in a blues club, but thought she was the wrong singer for them. After auditioning countless no-hopers, they decided to give her a try, and Joplin's performance, in which she seemed to drop all artifice and plug into a frighteningly deep source of raw emotion, more than won them over.

There seems little point in rehearsing the facts and figures of Joplin's drug use here, although it might serve to attempt to place it in perspective. At this remove, Joplin's prodigious capacity for quantities of heroin that frequently knocked out friends who fixed up with her might seem like little more than slow-motion suicide. But in the early 1960s, when Joplin first arrived in San Francisco, the drug culture was in its first blossoming. LSD was still legal in America, although soon to be criminalized, and heroin was seen as a harder drug in a range of drugs which were as popular as alcohol and tobacco, perhaps more so, among hip city dwellers. While heroin was illegal (yet in plentiful supply), it had not been demonized as it would be later, when, paradoxically, Joplin's own death would contribute to a change in attitudes towards heroin. (Joplin died on 4 October 1971, three weeks after Jimi Hendrix. A fanciful passage in Amburn's *Pearl* has Jim Morrison warning a friend, 'You're drinking with number three.')

What is worth rehearsing here, however, is Joplin's attitude to her own sexuality. Whatever her insecurities about relationships with either sex, Joplin does not appear to have had any qualms about her lesbian feelings. Not only did she pursue same-sex relationships with passion, she did not care who knew about them or indeed who observed her lesbian relationships. She expressed physical affection in public, once, notoriously, fondling Peggy Caserta's breasts during a press conference prior to her appearance at Woodstock. And her lesbianism was public enough, according to Caserta, for Smokey Robinson to dedicate a song to 'Janis and her lady' from the stage of a concert he gave in San Francisco.

It is equally possible that everyone was too stoned to notice, but Joplin doesn't appear to have suffered any loss of face or popularity for her queer behaviour. It is also possible that, in what was still the queerest town on Earth, being a dyke was cool as far as the flower children of Haight Ashbury and environs were concerned. (Which would make them rather different from their sexist and frequently homophobic British counterparts.) It is true that most of Joplin's recorded material, when it refers to gender, names a man as the object of the singer's desire, needs, frustration or anger. I would say that this is simply blues tradition, and that furthermore a corporation like CBS would not allow an artist to record a queer blues. It is also the case that Joplin wrote very little of her own material, relying on standards and the material of bands and friends, such as Kristofferson. (Kristofferson's own authorship of the male-identified 'Me and Bobby McGee' points to the pitfalls of simplistic analysis of gender roles in pop songs.)

As Gillian Gaar suggests, it is just as likely that Joplin was the victim of society's inability to deal with unconventional women as she was the victim of a particularly pure and potent overdose of heroin. There was no women's movement to support Joplin, and certainly no feminist theory that could cut its way through the thicket of beatnik jive, counterculture babble and the romantic notion of the rock star as doomed genius prevalent at the time. There were no role models for Joplin, save such tragic figures as Billie Holiday and Bessie Smith. As can be seen in the example of her contemporary (and, according to some reports, occasional drunken sparring partner) Jim Morrison, not only did 1960s rock stars think they should behave like this, but everyone else – media, managers, labels, fans – told them that they should behave like this. Given such a climate, it is no surprise that Janis Joplin partied right over the edge.

If Joplin was a victim of the era in which she lived, her story is with us today thanks to that era. When she died alone of a heroin overdose in a Los Angeles hotel, the first and until recently last out dyke in pop died with her. Today, a figure like Joplin would have two decades of feminism to rely on, a media that might be able to approach her on her own terms, a music industry that has (reluctantly) grown used to marketing unconventional women, and an audience that would be more sympathetic to her complexities.

Except, of course, Janis Joplin would not happen today, and since her death there has been an echoing silence around the subject of lesbians and pop. No other woman performer has felt able to match Joplin's perhaps careless candour, and I know of at least one promising career that has been ruined because of this. It would take nearly two decades before another woman could be outspoken about her life as a lesbian in pop.

Chapter ten

Walk Like a Woman, Talk Like a Man

JANIS Joplin had no gay male counterpart in the 1960s, a fact that makes her candour seem even more like a queer badge of courage. Male pop stars indulged in all manner of role play and verbal games with the media, some of which carried a muted queer subtext, but none would be particularly overt until David Bowie erupted on the scene at the end of the decade. Mick Jagger's posturing invited and received homophobic abuse, as well as homophile delight, notably the famous comments by the outrageously out gay MP Tom Driberg about his fascination with Jagger's crotch. In America, Jim Morrison had taken male (hetero)sexuality in rock as far as the law would allow and then beyond that barrier, getting himself arrested for the act of exposure onstage in Miami, an event which led to his departure for Europe shortly before his death in Paris in 1971. (Writer/activist Jim Fouratt does claim, however, in Martin Duberman's *Stonewall*, to have had a week-long fling with Jim Morrison in the late 1960s.)

Both Jagger and Morrison have been hailed for their sexual ambiguity, although at this remove it is difficult to discern anything but heterosexual themes in any of their recordings, performances or statements. It might be the case, however, that Jagger, aware of the British class system and the interlocking hierarchy of gender and sexual identity, realized that by borrowing some of the techniques of black rhythm and blues performers he could scandalize the media, who were every aspiring pop star's conduit to a large public. Any queer subtext that might be teased out of 1960s pop music, fashions and marketing would have been in the form of coded appeals to homosexual fantasies. Like film stars, pop stars were and will forever be presented as screens on to which consumers can project their desires. If the appeal of pop stars could encompass queer consumers as well as the mainstream, so much the better, as long as no visible concessions were made to the homo subculture. Since the invention and marketing of the teenager, pop iconography and queer culture had begun to converge, anyway (the early 1960s film *Motorcycle Boys* straddles *The Wild One* and *Victim*, and revolves around a – frustrated – homoerotic relationship between two rockers which is revealed only towards the end of the film) and ever since there has been a queer subtext embedded in much popular culture. Quite often, this has been fed, written or created by gay men working in the field, although it has necessarily been vague, nebulous (the trick being to sell potentially hostile consumers queer culture without their fully realizing just how queer it is). As trends shift, change and mutate, there remains an uneasy standoff between queer art and the mainstream, a symbiosis marked by mistrust and fear: they may need each other, but that doesn't necessarily mean that they like each other.

For much 1960s pop consumerism, this was buried so deep in popular culture that very few, if any, consumers would have noticed. Biker culture, like mod and skinhead culture, carried aspects, accessories, or just hints of homosexual culture, but did so without the faintest hint of irony or parody. Gay culture, such as it was, was so underground, and when it came overground seemed to many to be associated with men of a certain age, class and cultural background, as to seem very remote from the mainstream. The tabloid media and popular culture may have encoded certain aspects of pop music – the falsetto voice, flamboyant emotional display, so-called effeminacy in terms of clothes, hair, accessories, makeup – with that curious English music-hall sense of poovery, which was at once both taboo and entertaining (witness the success of *Round the Horne's* Julian and Sandy, still to be outdone by Julian Clary thirty years on), but it would still take until the end of the decade before explicit homosexuality would make its presence felt in pop and rock. Even the much-touted decadence of the Velvet Underground (who took their name from a dimwitted and pedestrian pseudo-scientific survey of kinky sex in the suburbs) and their cohorts in Andy Warhol's Factory was only really established after the event. In the case of the Velvet Underground, it is important to remember that, however the passage of time may have exaggerated their legendary status, the true Velvet Underground existed only for a year or two, recorded two albums, played very little, and never visited Britain or any other countries outside the United States. If the Velvet Underground had any cool among their contemporaries, it was as people who were very probably drug addicts.

Some 1960s pop did stray into queer territory, most famously The Kinks' 'Lola', Ray Davies's (probably autobiographical) song about a visit to a trannie nightclub during which the narrator finds himself uncharacteristically drawn into an area of sexuality he had never before encountered (a theme that would recur elsewhere, for me most notably in Randy Newman's 'Half a Man'). While the narrator indulges in illicit sex with Lola, he still seems to insist that he 'don't understand' why she walked like a woman but talked like a man. (Powerful echoes, here, of 'Sissy Man Blues' and other queer blues.) As a piece of songwriterly reporting, it's the equivalent of a vicarious trip to the Rieperbahn or Amsterdam's red-light district. Similarly, Pink Floyd's 'Arnold Layne' is famously said to be about cross-dressing and associated pleasures, although the song itself is so densely psychedelic as to resist all but the most tenuous of interpretations.

There were also, despite the fact that they remained almost totally hidden from public gaze, homosexual performers in rock and pop in the 1960s. Most noteworthy is veteran blues singer and bandleader Long John Baldry, nicknamed for his 6 foot and 7 inches height. Baldry was one of the fathers of the British blues boom of the early 1960s, alongside such figures as Alexis Korner, John Mayall and Graham Bond. He sang in Korner's original Blues Incorporated, and later with the Cyril Davies band. When Davies died in 1964, Baldry took over as bandleader, renaming the group the Hoochie Coochie Men. He also introduced a young friend, Rod Stewart, as second singer in the band.

That same year, tiring of having to run the Hoochie Coochie

Men, Baldry joined organist Brian Auger's new line-up, the soon-to-become-legendary rhythm and blues revue band Steampacket, taking Stewart with him, and joining producer Giorgio Gomelsky's secretary, a young singer by the name of Julie Driscoll, in the vocal frontline. Auger is quoted in at least one rock encyclopedia as saying that Baldry was 'the greatest white blues singer of the period'.

Stewart's and Baldry's careers diverged shortly afterwards, the former leaving to develop his own career with Shotgun Express, and later the Jeff Beck Group and, of course, The (Small) Faces. Baldry launched his own Bluesology, which boasted a young pianist, Reg Dwight, and a saxophonist, Elton Dean. When the pianist decided to launch his own solo career, a passage in Philip Norman's *Elton John* records that Dwight first asked saxophonist Dean, now a leading light of the European jazz avant-garde, if he could borrow his name wholesale. Dean told him, quite bluntly, that he couldn't. (To this day, Dean blushes when ribbed about this story.) Dwight tiptoed off with the Christian names of his boss and his boss's saxophonist, reversed them, and later changed his name from Reg Dwight to Elton John by deed poll. (The most newsworthy thing about Elton John's homosexuality, masked first by fake weddings, then the 'actually-I'm-bi' clause, was that for decades we were all looking in the wrong direction. While speculation rested on the Elton John–Bernie Taupin relationship, John was, at least in the early days of his career, living with manager John Reid.)

Baldry had a chart hit in 1967 with 'Let the Heartaches Begin', although this schmaltzy ballad saw a turning-point in his career, away from raw rhythm and blues and towards a smoother and lighter style. Baldry subsequently worked in the cabaret circuit, but disenchanted with the English music scene he emigrated to Vancouver, where he is based today. He fronts his own rock/blues unit, which toured Britain in 1993. He has been out about his homosexuality for many many years – indeed, friends from the early 1960s say that Baldry was never in in the first place. While rumour and fact attach themselves to a number of other 1960s pop figures, it is worth remembering that a key figure in the British blues boom – which, after all, begat the whole hard rock/heavy metal scene, that fount of everything macho in pop and rock today – was a fairy the size of a Watusi.

Another pop figure from the 1960s who is now known to have been gay is Billy Fury, one of the many Elvis Presley clones that were factory farmed by the British music industry in the wake of rock'n'roll. Unlike many of his contemporaries, however, Fury did actually write a number of his remarkable nineteen chart hits. At this remove, however, Fury is probably more memorable for the fact that he was managed by queer entrepreneur Larry Parnes than for his impact on the history of rock'n'roll.

If the arid, pre-1967 Sexual Offences Act 1960s pop scene seemed absolutely heterosexual, it was also remarkable for the advent of the gay manager/producer in pop. While one can also make a case for the pre-eminence of heterosexual pop entrepreneurs, it is noteworthy that a quartet of gay men – Larry Parnes, Joe Meek, Kit Lambert and Brian Epstein – were so instrumental in the birth and development of British pop.

This is a difficult area for the queer hack (or at least this queer hack). Managers are necessarily unpleasant people. They need to be to protect the interests of their charges, and to get where they want to get to in the business. Heterosexual managers are also monsters – one thinks of Allen Klein, who presided over the disintegration of the Beatle empire – but it is hard to find any factors in the lives of this quartet that might lend themselves to the notion of queer hero or role model. Nor, really, can one find any redeeming features in the public image of their inheritors, such figures as Jonathan King (The Weathermen, Piglets, himself), Tam Paton (Bay City Rollers), Simon Napier-Bell (Wham!, Tom Robinson, briefly, and queer popsters A Blue Mercedes) and Tom Watson (Pet Shop Boys until 1989, East 17, and the man who broke new ground when he told *The Word* that aspiring young pop things had to be good in bed – his bed).

There should be no surprise in the fact that people like Parnes or his successors should have become involved in the music industry. Clever, talented and ambitious gay men inevitably gravitate towards the professions where they are most likely to find acceptance and fulfilment. As Jon Savage notes in *England's*

Dreaming, his epic history of the Sex Pistols and punk rock, the history of pop 'is full of interactions between middle-class, often Jewish, often homosexual entrepreneurs and working-class male performers'.

If sex wasn't involved, Jon Savage continues, then quite often these entrepreneurs enjoyed a vicarious celebrity through the career of their charges. While many of his charges were poor shadows of the American artists they aped, Larry Parnes was responsible for the careers of Joe Brown, Marty Wilde and Georgie Fame, and he created a successful template for the invention and marketing of pop stars. Producer Joe Meek, famous for recording 'Telstar' and other hits in his tiny flat on the Holloway Road in north London, invented the bright, trebly sound that dominated 1960s Britbeat. Meek's death was surrounded by Ortonesque tragedy; after a bizarre disagreement, he murdered his landlady and then committed suicide. Kit Lambert, son of Constant, one of the composers who had ridiculed the queer Benjamin Britten, managed The Who through their most productive period in the mid- to late-1960s. In 1981, Lambert died after falling down a flight of stairs, an accident that was believed to have been caused by a life-threatening mixture of alcohol and drugs. During the period that Lambert managed The Who, they produced virtually all their classic singles: 'I Can't Explain', 'My Generation', 'Substitute', 'I'm a Boy', 'Happy Jack', 'Pictures of Lily' and 'I Can See for Miles'. The career of Beatles manager Brian Epstein needs no elaboration here.

Mod, the movement for whom The Who acted as house band, might be considered the youth culture where pop and queer crossed over. The original 'modernists', mythically sited in Colin MacInnes's Notting Hill, were sharp-dressing pill-popping hipsters who smoked Gitanes, read Sartre and listened to John Coltrane (or so the myth had it). The high street model, however, was more mundane, if no less addicted to the pharmaceutical pleasures of purple hearts, black bombers and (as the myth also had it) aspirin dropped into Coca-Cola. These were the two-tone suited tearaways who donned parkas and mounted their Vespas to become folk devils on the beaches of Brighton, Southend and Margate.

Memoirs from the era written by the likes of Peter Burton and Derek Jarman suggest that, in the urban in-crowd, there was a cross-over between mod culture and queer culture. Again, I would say that this would probably have occurred only in the rarefied circles of arty, intellectual London, and would not have filtered down to the high street, except in the most anonymously coded form. My parents had one of these folk devils at home, the same older brother who had been obsessed about the work of Elvis Presley. He once confided in me that he carried a chain whenever there was a chance that he and his mod friends were at risk of attack by their mortal enemies, the rockers. The first queer he ever met was me.

Queer culture itself began to adopt a more public profile during the 1960s, in literature, theatre and film, and with first the Wolfenden Report and then the campaign by the likes of MP Leo Abse to get the 1967 Sexual Offences Act passed – a campaign attended by vitriolic anti-gay comment in the media. Following the example of the Mattachine Society in America, the Albany Society, named after the West End enclave where this group of proto-gay-rights-activists met, and the North-West Campaign for Homosexual Equality, the Mancunian organization that would drop its regional prefix when its campaign became nationwide in the 1970s, both began agitating for homosexual rights in the wake of 1967. Little of this translated into the gay subculture, less still into pop. When the counter-culture declared war on the establishment, however, all this would change, but only after a fight. The counterculture in Britain was never very pro-gay, so counterculture queers set up their own communities, like Bethnal Rouge and the GLF squat in Railton Road, Brixton. One of the editors of *Oz* magazine, Jim Anderson, was queer, but that didn't stop the magazine from publishing drug-crazed homophobic rants and prurient features about the homo underworld. (With few exceptions, its staff have gone on to become darlings of the right or coked-out me-generation libertarians. I've worked with some of them.) As with the world of the far left, who had a macho thing about beating up fairies who tried to join their demonstrations, it would take shock treatment to change this. And funnily enough, it was a breeder who applied the electrodes.

Chapter eleven

Dire Straights: Ziggy, Iggy, Marc, Lou

IF history has any sense of justice, it will record the fact that the first pop star to cause a controversy by publicly asserting his homosexuality was, irony of ironies, heterosexual all along.

David Bowie didn't even think up the wheeze of coming out as gay as a means of heightening his public profile. That was down to his manager, Ken Pitt, who, in 1969, following the success of 'Space Oddity', began to court the embryonic British gay media (meaning, by and large, the magazine *Jeremy*). Intriguingly, this actually predates the arrival in Britain in 1970 of the concept of gay liberation, imported from America where it came into being during the aftershocks of the Stonewall riots of July 1969. The *Jeremy* article, which appeared in January 1970, is an unremarkable and wholly anodyne piece, a rather detached observation of Bowie's Queen Elizabeth Hall concert, a chat with Bowie at home in Beckenham, and a promotional appearance at the Speakeasy. Nothing controversial, not even a hint of sexuality, was discussed. But for an artist even to contemplate talking to 'the gay press' (as we never really called it until the late 1970s or early 1980s) in 1970 was itself a radical act, and could only have started pushing buttons with a gay audience starved of contemporary queer culture.

It wasn't until 1972, in an interview with *Melody Maker* writer Michael Watts, that Bowie 'came out' as gay. By then, with the sleeves to *The Man Who Sold the World* (David in full-length frock and floppy hat) and *Hunky Dory* (David in glam outfit with generous helping of salami down right trouser leg) to hand, you didn't need to be Roland Barthes to decode the public persona that David Bowie was projecting. Although maybe you did: Barthes might have picked up on the subtext of artifice and performance that everyone else seemed to overlook at the time.

A consummate self-publicist from the outset, Bowie must have realized he was handing Michael Watts a scoop on a golden platter, although Watts appears to have been the first journalist to question Bowie directly about his sexuality. 'Yes, of course I'm gay, and always have been,' Bowie told Watts. At the same time, according to Jerry Hopkins's book, *Bowie*, he was assuring his mother, 'Don't believe a word of it, mum.'

David Bowie the 'out' gay was just another role for Bowie, who wasn't, of course, even David Bowie, really, but David Jones of south London playing at being a media star called David Bowie. Bowie constructed this myth assiduously, for a while running with a gay crowd, saying things to the media like (to *Rolling Stone*) 'your readers can make up their minds about me when I begin getting adverse publicity; when I'm found in bed with Raquel Welch's husband.' As we now know, David Bowie was more likely to be found in bed with Raquel Welch than with her husband, but such deft, casual gobbets of scandal were the lifeblood that kept the myth of Queer David alive. Indeed, while Bowie long ago dropped the pretence of even bisexuality, an aura of queerness has clung to him to the extent that he is probably the only heterosexual on the planet who has so much space devoted to him in the world's gay media. Bowie has no equal as a bricoleur and self-mythifier. The atmosphere of do-it-yourself legend-writing around Bowie is extraordinary. Early in the 1970s, then-manager Tony DeFries told Bowie to start telling the press that he was preparing for the lead part in a film of Robert Heinlein's novel *Stranger in a Strange Land*, assuring Bowie that the scripts would soon start turning up in the post. Sure enough, the scripts duly began arriving, although the film was never made (or even begun). Similarly, at another point in the 1970s Bowie was 'doing' Orwell's *1984* for TV. This despite the fact that Orwell's widow Sonia had repeatedly refused to discuss any such project (she hated the earlier British TV treatment, apparently). Still, to quote his friend David Byrne, monkey speak, monkey do, and I don't think there is anything you could teach Bowie about guerrilla semiotics. He confessed to *Rolling Stone*, 'I am an awful liar,' and who could blame him? Telling fibs to the press became a cargo cult, and one where the great silver bird actually did land, disgorging armies of journalists whose quotes from the ever-quotable David Bowie would bring planeloads of other journalists, and so on.

Long after he had come out as heterosexual, Bowie was still stoking the Queer David myth with genderfuck imagery in videos ('Boys Keeping Swinging') and on album sleeves (*Scary Monsters*), almost as though keeping it alive, feeding his Frankenstein's monster. Despite all this, and despite his coked-out dalliance with fascism in the 1970s (which still dogs him: as late as 1988, I stood in a Bowie audience in London and watched a theatre full of Bowie fanatics throwing him Nazi salutes), it is hard to totally hate David Bowie for this. For all the play-acting, for all the fraudulent posing, David Bowie presided, unwittingly I believe, over a sea-change in social attitudes. I say 'preside' (which can mean in the chair, at the head, superintending, acting as a tutelary god or, with droll coincidence, to be at the piano or organ) because ascribing social change to pop stars is as dubious as the myth popular in the late 1960s and early 1970s which held that Dirk Bogarde's performance in *Victim* brought about the changes in the 1967 Sexual Offences Act.

As the Queer David myth developed through the 1970s, with the landmark *Ziggy Stardust and the Spiders from Mars* album and, later, *Diamond Dogs*, Bowie in fact lived with a succession of girlfriends. If this irony failed to impress itself on the headline-happy mainstream press, there should be no real surprise in the fact that it bypassed the alternative press as well. In 1972, the in-house newspaper of the new gay subculture, *Gay News*, commented, 'David Bowie is probably the best rock musician in Britain now. One day he'll become as popular as he deserves to be. And that'll give gay rock a potent spokesman.' Or maybe not: Queer David had in fact told Michael Watts that he 'despised' the gay liberation movement, although he obviously adored their frocks.

It took a couple of heterosexual American critics to begin asking pertinent questions about Bowie's sexuality. Cameron Crowe, of *Rolling Stone* and *Playboy*, quoted Bowie as saying that

American women frequently tried to persuade him that heterosexual sex wasn't so bad. When he was approached in this manner, Queer David would 'just play dumb' (i.e., go to bed with them). It took the irascible and, these days, rather dead Lester Bangs to comment, zeroing in on Bowie's fear of flying, 'I always thought all that Ziggy Stardust homo-from-Aldebaran was a crock of shit, especially coming from a guy who wouldn't even get in a goddam airplane.'

And yet in Britain at least the Queer David myth persisted, and maybe even took on a religious sheen. Newspaper print plants appeared to have been programmed to append the prefix 'outrageous bisexual' to every mention of David Bowie's name. His diehard fans, ossified in whatever era of Bowie's development that meant the most to them, still appeared at his concerts decked out in the Bowie drag of that era. Despite his quite distasteful statements about Hitler being the first rock star, his appearance at Victoria Station in 1976 with outriders and star in suprematist panoply, and his comments that Britain might benefit from a dictatorship, many, and probably most, sensible liberal journalists still adored Bowie unquestioningly. And despite all the available evidence, the gay subculture and its media still regarded David Bowie as the nearest thing to a queer pope ('the spice of his image,' writes gay critic Jon Savage, 'was his gayness'). The (inter)national obsession with David Bowie defied, and defies, logic.

By this time, of course, the damage had been done. Ushering in a battalion of imitators, opportunists and bandwagoneers, Bowie declared open season on gender roles. Coinciding, quite happily for him, with gay lib, women's lib, and the turmoil and upheaval of the early 1970s, economic, political and global, be it the three-day week, the miners' strike or the war in Vietnam, Bowie took centre stage in a near-vacuum and held on to it. The only other youth cult that might have competed with the glam rock revolution that grew up around Bowie was the short-lived skinhead cult that flared at the turn of the decade, a minority distinguished by its violence, expensive taste in clothes (two-tone mohairs, Levis, Ben Sherman shirts, Doc Martens, brogues), and, paradoxically considering they were racist, a taste for Jamaican reggae (which at least gave us the Upsetters, The Cats' 'Swan Lake in Reggae' and the *Tighten Up* compilations). The cost of dressing skinhead was too much, and the violence too much to stomach, for most teenagers of the time, and skinheads moved into the margins, joining the demonology of outsiders – teds, greasers – who terrorized the mainstream, which could be roughly divided into two: the longhairs who listened to 'progressive' rock, and the smoothies who dressed in the fashions of the time (satin jackets, ballooning flares and stacked heels being a fairly typical example).

As someone who left school aged fifteen, the year David Bowie released *Hunky Dory*, I belong to a generation that probably has to thank Queer David for the comparative ease with which we came out. However outrageous the model, Queer David was blessed with the glow of celebrity, which got him into the *Daily Mirror* and on to the Russell Harty Show, and at a time when queer appearances in the media tended to be in the form of arrests and police statistics. Michel Foucault would probably disapprove, but Queer David's clever (if ultimately meaningless) packaging of sexual outrage created a safe space where many of us, gay, bi or straight, could play out games and experiment with difference, finding ourselves and going through the motions of teenage rebellion, in a way that not even punk could imitate.

It is probably important to define Queer David's role further. He did not necessarily help shape my sexuality – I was already cottaging when *Hunky Dory* was released, and dating an older guy by the time *Ziggy Stardust* appeared – or, necessarily, anyone else's, but his high-profile example created a breathing space both for queers and for those who weren't sure about their sexuality or their feelings about the sexuality of others. I knew and know heterosexuals whose attitudes about sexual difference were radically altered by the atmosphere of glam rock, particularly by the field of ambiguity staked out by David Bowie. Many questioned their own attitudes to sexuality, some to the extent of exploring their own bisexual potential, and others began to rethink their prejudices about sexual difference. Quite often this was brought about by the fact that their favourite music was being produced by a queer: a simplistic way to overturn a prejudice but, as was the case with Tom Robinson, Culture Club, the Bronskis and Frankie years later, meeting one you like does seem to work.

With the possible exception of Iggy Pop, whom I once saw partying with a gaggle of adoring gay teenagers on the road in Germany, the rest of Bowie's accomplices in glam – Marc Bolan, happily married to June, Lou Reed, another self-mythifier whose queer work was fiction (and also now happily married), and the pouting peacock from Roxy Music, Brian Eno, whose idea of a fun video (*Thursday Afternoon*) is a fixed camera filming his girlfriend rolling around in the bath – also appear to have been resolutely heterosexual throughout the period, regardless of the clothes, and regardless of the wasted tonnages in foundation, panstick, lip gloss and eyeliner. As critic Barry Lazell has said, David Bowie intended to signify Ziggy Stardust, not *be* him. So, too, did the serried ranks of glamrockers, breeders to a man, intend to signify sexual ambiguity, difference and danger, while preferring to clock off at the end of the day and pop home to the wife and kids. (There was never any question that Slade, Sweet or Gary Glitter, the original Bacofoil turkey, were ever anything but heterosexual.) That gay men should subscribe to this culture seems to have been largely incidental to the real business of shocking our parents: as Lester Bangs wrote in 1975, 'Everybody knows faggots don't like David Bowie and the [New York] Dolls – that's for teenagers and pathophiles [he means sociopaths]. Faggots like musical comedies and soul music.'

At least Bangs pays faggots the compliment of good taste in soul music, although what's at work here is multiple myth-making. Bangs and his pals – 'sociopaths', misunderstood James Deans to a man – were hip and naughty enough to like Bowie and 'the Dolls' (spot the tribal abbreviation), while faggots were so beyond the pale they listened to Stephen Sondheim, Barbra Streisand, Donna Summer. Bangs wheels out one tired old myth to shore up his own romantic myth of himself. Of course, neither myth is true.

While any pop cult can expect its followers to imitate its modes of dress and behaviour, I don't think anyone could have expected so much feedback to occur as it did with glam. Pop had always been about rebellion, however illusory, and about sex, but the complex patterns of cause and effect went far beyond this in the early 1970s. With glam, it went still one step further, with young males dressing and decorating themselves in a way that might invite derision and actual assault from peers who subscribed to other fashions, and the cause of that derision or assault would be the notion of masculinity and how contemporary fashion was undermining that notion. If the late 1960s and early 1970s were the years where long hair on men was sometimes enough to occasion physical assault, the glam years were a period when young men sometimes willingly risked homophobic assault by dressing in the manner of their pop idol, even if they themselves weren't homosexual.

In Britain, this coincided with the burgeoning gay scene, and the two worlds blurred into each other. The new, if tentative, confidence among gay men, built on the harmless but mistaken assumption that the 1967 Sexual Offences Act legitimized the homosexual lifestyle, saw a new form of gay nightlife appear at clubs like The Catacombs in Earls Court and Chaguarama's in Kensington, both of them hangouts for hip heterosexuals as well as their gay clientèle.

For a number of years in the early 1970s (we might date it up to the ascendancy of disco) there was a busy cross-traffic between gay fashions (in music, in dress, in drugs, in other cultural apparel; films, books, design, nightlife, travel) and rock fashions. The traffic was largely one way, with rock fashion picking up on queer trends (radical drag, as seen in the Lindsay Kemp mime troupe, was after all what inspired Bowie to cross-dress and play at genderfuck, and the tradition continued with such disparate gay spectacles as La Grande Eugene, the Cycle Sluts, and Hot Peaches). There would be queer influences on punk, but, like the trend itself, these would be avant-garde rather than populist.

This was probably one of the easiest periods in history in which to come out as lesbian or gay, even though, as Ron Peck's film *Nighthawks* painfully reminds us, we did it in flares. In London, at least, to be openly gay on the streets – with Campaign for Homosexual Equality badges, badges that said 'Dykes/Faggots Ignite!', and 'How Dare You Presume I'm Heterosexual?', by holding hands or kissing in public – had none of the political (or criminal) meaning it has in the 1990s. There was a risk of queerbashing, but even that was minor compared to the potential for homophobic violence today. Being out at work, with family, neighbours, friends, was an altogether simpler thing to do than it is today, when the constant drone of the right-wing press, explicit anti-queer campaigns such as Clause 28, and the no less explicit demonology of AIDS, have in some instances figured gay men as murderous plague carriers. Thirteen years of Thatcherism and the monster's legacy have left Britain a very different place to what it was in 1979.

In all probability, there were other social forces at work – movements to change legislation on abortion, divorce, women's and children's rights, access to contraception and sex education, welfare benefits campaigns – which would have carried lesbian and gay rights along with them, although as many will attest, the early 1970s were not an easy time to be queer and left-wing in Britain.

None of these movements, however, would have had the impact on youth culture, and that culture's knock-on effect on society in general, as Queer David and the breeders from Mars. But it is unlikely that any of them realized the effect they were having, or that they might even care. David Bowie eventually recanted the sub-Futurist fascination with totalitarian politics which once saw him superimposed next to Enoch Powell and Adolf Hitler on Rock Against Racism posters. He even played at Live Aid (suggesting, crassly, that they make it an annual affair!) and the Freddie Mercury 'tribute'. A journalist who got an in-depth interview with Bowie in the late 1970s came away thinking that Bowie was neither left- or right-wing but spookily amoral and utterly self-absorbed. It is even possible that behind all that slap and Bette Davis drag, David Jones is in fact a homophobe: his idea of oppositional sexuality is a decadent cliché borrowed from the blurbs of paperback Genet, Burroughs and Hubert Selby Jnr. Queer David inhabited a universe peopled by beautiful criminals, outrageous drag queens, mugwumps, wild boys. Not much space there for the sort of queer you might find in David Leavitt or Adam Mars-Jones. But, wittingly or unwittingly, Queer David set the stage for real queers to start singing about themselves in pop songs.

Chapter twelve

The Winter of '79 Revisited

ON Saturday, 13 August 1977, an overcast day in London, a small group of National Front members and supporters gathered in Fordham Park in New Cross, south London, in preparation for what had been described as an 'anti-mugging' march through New Cross and Lewisham. The march was intended solely to menace the area's large African–Caribbean, Asian and Mediterranean communities (they were the 'muggers' the fascists were 'marching' against) and garner some publicity for the NF.

An estimated five thousand protesters turned up to stop the NF that day. They milled around on the New Cross Road, determined to block the NF's route out of the park and on to Lewisham. The police, who probably outnumbered the fascist marchers five to one, attempted to get the march moving three times, but each time the crowd of anti-fascist protesters, swarming around Clifton Rise, the road running from Fordham Park on to the New Cross Road, would surge to halt them. I and a friend, Julian, had attended the official anti-fascist demonstration, in nearby Ladywell, and the march to New Cross. Standing quite near the front of the crowd at the top of Clifton Rise, we agreed, sensible cowards both of us, that we would make our excuses and leave if things turned nasty. As it turned out, we weren't given much of a choice.

On the fourth attempt to get the NF out of the park, a senior police officer came up to the crowd and warned us that we might be injured if we did not get out of the way. Julian and I began scouting our exit route, but at that moment the mounted police cantered into view and we found ourselves arms linked with the front line of the crowd. A ridiculous moment of social embarrassment – how *do* you extricate yourself from a demo when Rosa Luxemburg appears to have hold of one arm, and Daniel Cohn-Bendit the other? – pitched us into what looked like revolutionary bravery on television later that day, although it didn't feel much like it as the cops kicked and shoved us out of the way of a hundred or so NF marchers.

The horses drove a wedge into the crowd, followed by cops on foot who pushed us backwards up Clifton Rise, across the New Cross Road and, in our case, backwards over the front garden wall of a house facing the Rise. Some people took refuge in doorways, others proceeded to pelt the police and fascists with whatever they could lay their hands on; pebbles and stones from gardens, bits of brick and concrete broken off walls.

'Suddenly the sky darkened,' wrote the late David Widgery in his history of the Rock Against Racism movement, *Beating Time*. Unfortunately, the projectiles that Widgery was observing were hitting as many, if not more, anti-fascists as fascists and, indeed, the police who were there to protect them. The police got a dribble of the NF through, and a large part of the anti-fascist crowd followed them down into Lewisham, where running battles broke out between demonstrators and police. According to David Widgery, cowed fascist leader John Tyndall told supporters, 'I think the Third World War has just started out there.'

Many writers, musicians and activists of my generation were blooded at Lewisham, some literally. This was probably the first major demonstration in London since the big anti-Vietnam protests of the late 1960s. We hadn't seen before the frightening speed with which a demo can turn into a riot, nor had we seen the blatantly partisan behaviour of the Metropolitan Police. It was the nearest we might have got to a Siege of Chicago, although in truth it wasn't near the scale of the 1968 Democratic Convention riots at all. Still, as Widgery wrote, 'A lot came out of the events at Lewisham.' It saw the birth of the Anti-Nazi League, and pushed the nascent Rock Against Racism into a higher gear than at any time in the year since its inception. And, for the first time in south London, the communities who were being targeted by the fascists saw that whites, straight and gay, were also prepared to stand up to the bully boys.

Of all the images and events of the Rock Against Racism era, one image sticks in my memory more than most; more, certainly, than the subsequent anti-racist carnivals in Victoria and Brockwell parks. Minutes before the sky went dark over the New Cross Road, I caught a glimpse of the Tom Robinson Band – and they were there as a group, Robinson, guitarist Danny Kustow, keyboards player Mark Ambler, drummer Dolphin Taylor – sprinting past with Robinson at the front shouting that the police were about to bring the NF out of the park. The TRB disappeared into the melée, but the image of Robinson and friends hurrying to engage the opposition in meaningful debate stuck with me more than any subsequent political act by a rock musician or band, the Clash included. Where all subsequent agit-rock events would be tinged with the stain of self-publicity, the TRB went to New Cross as anonymous members of a crowd with the sole intention of helping to stop the NF march. It also seemed to impress others: Julie Burchill and Tony Parsons dedicated their bilious 'obituary' of rock'n'roll, *The Boy Looked at Johnny*, to, among others, 'the TRB and everyone else on the same side at Lewisham 1977'.

Lewisham 1977 was a very TRB event, prefiguring the political paranoia of a song that would become a Tom Robinson Band classic, 'The Winter of '79'. It was composed before 1979, but written as though looking back in hindsight at a year when 'the world we knew busted open wide'. The song may seem hopelessly romantic these days, with its scaremongering heroics about the jailing of gays and left-wingers, the return of National Service, the rise of the National Front, SAS surveillance of activists, institutionalized racial violence and worse. But it comes from a decade when three-day weeks and miners' strikes brought down governments, when high-ranking military figures were found to have proposed a military coup against a Labour government, when rumours of rationing were commonplace and when a Labour government put itself on a collision course with the trades union movement.

Neither Tom Robinson nor his followers could have anticipated the events of 24 April 1979, when the Conservative Party swept to power. If they thought that Jim Callaghan had been bad enough, Margaret Thatcher had a thing or ten up her sleeve to show them. By then, however, the TRB was on its last legs, and would in fact have split up before the start of the winter of 1979. Yet the TRB remain emblematic of all the hopes and fears of those old/young enough to have been around at the time. Their unflashy, pragmatic and commonsense attitude to politics, a far remove from the Clash's sten guns in Knightsbridge posturing, galvanized untold thousands into action.

In the welter of self-identified gay performers who have appeared since, it is easy to lose sight of Robinson's unique (I believe) position in pop history. More than any individual before him or any individual (so far) after him, Robinson has lived his life as a gay man in the full glare of the media. Jimmy Somerville, adorable hothead that he is, may be angry enough to get arrested on ACT UP demos, but even Somerville has retreated from the glare. Whatever Robinson chose to do, history forced him to do it in the street. There have been times when he might have preferred a lower profile, but he seems to realize that this is part of the price you pay for being Tom Robinson.

In 1994, RAR is dead, along with David Widgery, and Tom Robinson has been living with a woman, Sue, for over six years. They have a four-year-old son. Robinson says that he still defines himself as gay for his own personal and political reasons. In fact, he is probably bisexual, which explains why he is having a rewarding relationship with a member of the opposite sex, and why they decided to have a child together. He feels it is simpler, and more honest, still to call himself gay. To declare himself bisexual now would probably draw fire from almost every quarter. The 'debate' about Robinson's sexuality actually appears to have detached itself from its subject, become an independent thing, a text burbling happily away to itself in the pages of the tabloids.

'That was an area that got taken completely out of my hands,' he says today. 'I mean, I'm as gay as I've ever been. I still fancy men as opposed to women. Nothing's changed as far as that is concerned.'

He does not want his position on his sexuality to be taken as a criticism of bisexuality, although he admits 'Until I became labelled as a bisexual, I subscribed to the standard gay theology that bis were failed gays who had not come out properly, or who were too chicken to come out as gay. I think it's partly karma for my disbelief coming back to haunt me that that applied to me! I've discovered that there is such a thing as bisexuality, and it genuinely is quite a painful dilemma for people to find themselves in. But although I have a shared experience with those kind of people, I don't see that as a, dare I say, camp that I want to belong to, because I don't see any point in splintering our movement. It's bad enough being splintered into lesbian and gay. I'd rather say, no, I'm gay, I subscribe to this and I'm behind this, I've been fighting for these rights for twenty years and I'm not going to stop now.'

For the record, Robinson says that he and his partner first met at a benefit for Gay Switchboard, an organization Robinson has been involved with for many years. They began to see each other regularly, 'and eventually ended up falling in love. I could have fallen in love with a man, I could have fallen in love with a woman. You don't choose.'

This soon became public knowledge. Robinson's friends and supporters were bemused, some perplexed, others suspicious. His enemies, straight and gay, crowed. Worse was to come: Fleet Street subterfuge forced Robinson to go public with his story, and in Rupert Murdoch's *Sun*, of all places.

'So how did it come about that I found myself proclaiming my marital bliss in the pages of the *Sun*? You may well ask! I was in the situation where I was singing "Glad to be Gay" on stage every night and then coming home to a woman. I thought, this is hypocritical, and I certainly don't want to be outed about it. So in every interview I did I would say in passing that, as it happens, I live with a woman but I still count myself as gay, and so on. This went on quite happily for a couple of years, then suddenly *The People* read one of those articles and went, "What a great story!"'

The People doorstepped Robinson, his manager, his partner, and even tracked his father down on holiday in France. They all told *The People*, in Robinson's Anglo-Saxon usage, 'to fuck off!' Visiting his newsagents the following Sunday, Robinson found that he had in fact given *The People* a lengthy exclusive, cobbled together from old interviews. Where they couldn't cobble together old material, they invented, printing a screed of inaccurate factoids about Sue. Tom and Sue let that one go. Then *The People* heard that Sue was pregnant – 'God knows who grassed us up!' – and again asked for an interview. More Anglo-Saxon expletives were proffered. So *The People* went to print with a story claiming that Robinson was trying to keep his 'love child' secret for fear that it might alienate his gay audience. When their son was born, *The People* again asked for an interview and photographs of the offspring. Further Anglo-Saxonisms ensued. A contact tipped Robinson off that *The People* was preparing another fictional 'exclusive', 'a really nasty one this time'. Hoping to pre-empt *The People* piece, they prepared their own detailed statement and got a friend, photographer Jill Furmanovsky, to take a set of photographs for release to the media. The statement and pictures were released via a small photographic agency, and picked up by the *Sun*. Hardly the ideal situation, but it spiked *The People*'s guns.

'If I was me ten years ago,' says Robinson, 'and somebody else, reading that newspaper I'd think, "Fuck this! Why is he talking to the *Sun*? Why does he have to go on about his bloody baby? Is he trying to undo all the work he's done?" My hand was forced, to stop even worse stuff being printed. We just had to do a spoiler story.'

Language, as William Burroughs wrote in *Electronic Revolution*, is a virus from outer space. Like the Andromeda Strain, it breeds. Tabloid newspapers are its favourite breeding ground. The Family Robinson tale began to mutate.

'One paper decided we were married; from then on she's my wife. Another paper said I've switched from homosexuality to being heterosexual. Another heard I'd had psychotherapy and said I'd had psychotherapy to change my sexuality. Now, I've got to promote this new album [*Love over Rage*, released by Cooking Vinyl in spring 1994] and I've got to talk to the bastards. If any of them research the press cuttings all these lies will come out again, these factoids. Factoids seem to breed. And I'm as homosexual as I ever was!'

Unhappier still was the reaction from the lesbian and gay community. 'It was a bit like boxing a shadow, really, because nobody said anything to my face, so there was nothing I could rebut. Yet reverberations came back from people, saying, "Aren't you pissed off about what people are saying about you?" And I go, "What are they saying! What are they saying!" and they'd say, "Oh, I thought I read something in the *Pink Paper* a couple of months ago." I think it's mostly verbal. I do detect a noticeable lack of warmth, or reduction of warmth, from audiences in gay situations. Maybe it's just my paranoia. I think my stock within the lesbian and gay community is necessarily a bit lower.'

Tom Robinson and I have history, although of the purely professional, or comradely, kind. The TRB were the first band I ever reviewed as a rock journalist, for the now-defunct rock paper *Sounds*. If memory serves, Julie Burchill and I reviewed them in the same week. Burchill told the *NME* that the TRB were the future of rock'n'roll. In *The Boy Looked at Johnny*, she and/or Parsons wrote, 'Compared to the Tom Robinson Band, everyone else is wanking into the wind.' It was a simile she would reverse in later years. Personal contact aside, I believe the TRB, and its frontman, to have been crucial in the history of political popular music, part of a continuum that includes Woodie Guthrie, Bob Dylan (my most unfavourite rock star), the Weavers, Phil Ochs, Richie Havens, Gil Scott Heron, The Clash, Crass and Billy Bragg. I'd also add the Queercore movement to that continuum, and women performers like Ronnie Gilbert, Holly Near, Cris Williamson, Phranc, Michelle Shocked, Ova and the Feminist Improvising Group.

What is most striking about Robinson, however, is the extraordinary candour of his work, a candour that becomes all the more extraordinary when you compare his work to that of other gay performers, out or otherwise. On one level, songs like 'Martin' and '2-4-6-8 Motorway' are romantic, mythic, fictional songs that fit in with the tradition of English singer-songwriting that nurtured Robinson. 'Motorway' is also probably the finest road song ever produced by an English rock'n'roller. On another level entirely, Robinson also addresses the complexities of homosexual desire, as well as the experience of living as a homosexual in today's society. At no point does he feel the need to edit or censor, to evade the public gaze or nudge the bedroom door closed. Many of his songs use the language and devices of fiction, but they speak to real queer events and experiences. A totally public figure, Robinson can sing a conventional song hymning (however ironically) a brand of car ('Grey Cortina'), gay identity ('Glad to be Gay') or gay desire (his overt cover of Coward's covert 'Mad About the Boy'). While others (the Bronskis, Somerville, Erasure) have approached this level of candour, none have ever matched Robinson's honesty.

Like Somerville after him, Robinson was sometimes criticized for his politics, although often this was by individuals and bands who would have felt more comfortable if Robinson wasn't rocking the boat so much. Looking back, Robinson might have been quite isolated in the position he took, and helpless to resist political and sexual labelling by others. Yet he says he felt quite comfortable with who and what he was.

'You can't control the sensationalizing, but the great luxury any artist has starting out is the luxury of inventing themselves. I certainly invented myself within the work I was doing, and was happy with the results, to stand up and be counted, which is what I felt needed doing at the time. And as it said on the sleeve of *Power in the Darkness*, if we fail we have to face the scorn of tomorrow's generation, and in a sense that's what happened. We did! Brave words, and you have to stand by them!'

While he remains proud of what the TRB contributed to movements like Rock Against Racism, he has no illusions about the politicking of the era. People may have dismissed Bob Geldof's criticism of most punk posturing – Geldof was, after all, a cynical former *NME* hack – but they had to eat their words when Geldof launched Band Aid. 'He actually changed the world, quite literally. There was a global event that literally affected millions of lives, at his instigation. You saw then what he was on about; action, not words. He accomplished more in practical terms than the whole of punk rock one hundred times over.'

Fifteen years on, the winter of '79 now seems to have been a fanciful fiction when compared to events in the intervening years: the Falklands, Greenham, Cruise, the 1984 miners' strike, GCHQ, Clause 28, Iraq, the AIDS backlash. However real it may have seemed at the time, our paranoia may have been misplaced considering what was about to follow the real winter of 1979.

'It's easy to forget what a bloody horrible time it was,' Robinson counters. 'I'm not saying that today is a bunch of roses, but it depends very much on who you are and what view you have. If you happen to be in the unlucky 17 per cent unemployed, then life really can be a dung heap. On the other hand, for the other 83 per cent the quality of life probably isn't as bad as it was headed at the end of the seventies. The poor have got appallingly much poorer. But the time of the Callaghan government! You just go back to footage of the time and it reminds you. There was a real sense of despair and gloom. It was all falling apart, we'd been betrayed and stabbed in the back. Plus there was the NF becoming a political force, much like the BNP is now.

'There was plenty of cause for gloom. So all of us who felt apocalyptic at the time, and there were a lot of us, could be forgiven for doing so. If you are making pop music it has to reflect the mood of the times around you or it isn't pop music. If Clash and 999 and the various others, and TRB, gave voice to those sentiments, it was only because that was what people in the audience were feeling as well. It succeeded because it chimed with the way people felt.'

In hindsight, the winter of '79 seems part of a far more innocent era, politically and sexually, when issues were simpler, the problems obvious, the solutions within easy reach. Tom Robinson, however, feels that it was never that easy.

'There are a lot of paradoxes. Gay Pride, for example, is bigger than it's ever been. Mindboggling compared to the 1970s. Yet on the marches there are no chants, there's no political dimension at all. It's just a big party with a chance to do some cruising. And it's good that it isn't a political statement to the younger generation in the metropolis. While one mourns the militancy of one's youth' – he laughs self-deprecatingly – 'I'd much rather have the present situation where people are able to live open, fulfilled and happy lives, and get on with it, rather than go back to a situation where there was only a minority who were visible and incredibly right on and could pat ourselves on the back for all the things we did. It's great that there are mainstream ways it's coming across.'

To many, the difference between the winter of '79 and the winter of '94 would be marked by the death of socialism, the disappearance of a credible opposition, and in the growth of the religion of personal greed fostered by Thatcherism, perhaps the end of politics itself. Again, Robinson doesn't think things are so bleak.

'The failure is not just on the left. The right is riven and falling apart. It's more that the traditional left/right way of looking at things, dividing things into labour and capital, just doesn't seem so simple any more. Labour is actually some sweatshop in Korea, and the society that you know and live in is divided in different ways, along racial lines, gender lines, all kind of things that come into the melting pot. The old certainties about who was right and who wrong and who was doing who down don't seem to resonate in the same way. But maybe I'm missing the plot here. Having become comfortably bourgeois over the years you can't know, can you? But I think if I was still signing on as I was in 1977 on the kind of money you get on the Social now I'd probably have a very different perspective.'

J. K. Galbraith has a rather chilling theory about the failure of compassion in politics, the failure even of the theory that we should vote to do for others what we hope would be done for us in the same circumstances. Galbraith's 'culture of contentment' sees a newly affluent majority, in Britain the people who were sold shares and their own council houses by the Tories, abandoning all concern for the don't-haves, who are slowly becoming a silent and disenfranchised underclass. Tom Robinson counters Galbraith with Robert Hughes's theory of victim culture.

'There's also the culture of complaint, which puts another slant on that. That's true what Galbraith is saying. But against it there's also a culture of "Well, I ought to be given it. I deserve some money and somebody out there ought to give it to me, as my right." There's a sense that "they" ought to be looking after us.'

You believe that?

'Well, Robert Hughes suggests that victim status is becoming more and more sought after. It's not your "fault". Even white middle-class male powerbrokers are saying it: "My father was awful to me so I'm going out into the woods to bang drums, throw off the shadow of my father and find my manhood!" Rather than getting on with trying to change the external world.'

Lest a shade of libertarianism seem to be sneaking in here, he says, 'I start from a fundamental belief, the old "truth we hold as self-evident", that all people are created equal with equal rights. They're not the same, but different and equal. We do all have the right to live on the planet, and the right to respect from each other as human beings. Lesbian and gay rights, anti-racism and anti-sexism all spring from that basic belief.'

So what is a committed and concerned songwriter to do when faced with the complications of the post-modern world? Voltaire's notion of tending one's own garden grows more attractive by the day.

'Well, that's one alternative. People have tended to end up going into sexual politics and that, because that's an area where you can change something, and because they got so disheartened with trying to change the big issues, having failed massively. I think that's one reason why in America people got concerned with trying to change the attitudes and the language about how people interact with each other, because they can't seem to effect any change on Reaganomics or whatever. I've seen that expressed elsewhere and it seems to make sense.'

While moving into personal politics around attitudes and language may solve certain problems in the short term, there is also a suspicion that we are walking away from the bigger issues. Some, the so-called crusties, and the Dongas, who have dropped out to save trees and ancient common land, seem to have found a manageable way of negotiating the politics of their commitment. Yet it also seems to be undercut by a vein of despair.

'Well,' Robinson says, 'I've just made my bleakest album in years, and I hadn't realized until listening back to it how desolate I was feeling. I thought I was in quite a good humour and had quite a happy home life and all the rest of it, but the overall outlook isn't so great, is it?'

There are some things that Robinson does feel are improving, such as the situation of queers in pop, not to mention his own career, and his personal contentment. The upsurge of pop queers in the 1980s was, he says unequivocally, 'Fantastic! Turning on the telly and seeing Erasure on "Top of the Pops"! Bronski Beat! It was a huge elation. I was really pleased and proud, seeing what we thought we would never see. What really moved me was stuff like

Smash Hits or *Just 17* interviewing Andy Bell and not asking him about his sexuality, but asking him about his clothes and in the course of it him saying "My boyfriend this or my boyfriend that". Just taking for granted the fact that he's gay. To me, that's what gay liberation should always have been about.'

He is, however, reluctant to read too much into the way *Smash Hits* or *Just 17* treat Andy Bell's references to his boyfriend (which could just as easily be seen as ignoring the obvious in the hope that it simply fades away).

'We've got a long way to go, out there in Normal-land. It's easy living in the rarefied atmosphere of London's chattering classes, to imagine that social attitudes have changed. I'm sure any volunteer on Gay Switchboard will tell you it just ain't so, that they still get calls from people in Hull, Doncaster, Glasgow, Belfast, who think they're the only queer in the world and who suffer agonies at the hands of their contemporaries and mates. Attitudes are changing, and things are getting better, but there's still a lot of hatred and prejudice, and, what's the word? Superstition, almost, about it.'

While some of us daydream about acquiring the where-withal to flee, Robinson has not walked away from the big issues. His new album, *Love over Rage*, still tackles the big issues, including, on 'The Days That Changed the World', the fact that we have yet to change the world – even if we did Feed it a snack. His new album also addresses the subject of AIDS and the loss of friends to the syndrome. It took a while, he says, because it usually takes time for such major personal events to take on the perspective and proportions that make them manageable in song form.

Mostly, however, he says that his work nowadays is mainly about the nature of being a man. 'What interests me more than anything at present is the masculine condition, as opposed to the specifically gay condition or the heterosexual condition. I'm tending to classify myself just as a man now, and trying to sidestep the whole business of one having to be this kind of male, because I have a much more common experience now with most of the men I come across.'

Asked to explain this, he says that presenting 'The Locker Room' for BBC Radio Four, he has to interview a great many men about their masculinity, and he has found that under the skin he feels a lot in common with his interview subjects. Most gay men would site the source of their oppression in the hostile reactions of heterosexual men, but Robinson says, 'I found that being openly gay all along made a huge difference in that way, in that people who might have been homophobic would not have been my friends in the first place.'

His career has taken a different tack since the mid-1980s hits with 'War Baby' and 'Atmospherics', and even though it has been low-key for some time that too has its compensations. The periods when the TRB were embarking on high-profile, large-venue tours and recording albums with big budgets and big-name producers, were, he says, not particularly happy times for him personally. Robinson now works in the manner of Robert Fripp's 'small, mobile unit', and put this new album together for a budget of just £16,000 – a fraction of the cost that large-label albums incur. Working in this fashion has, he says, 'been an unexpected compensation and bonus. I'd be lying through my teeth to say I wouldn't like to be on "Top of the Pops" or signed to Sony, that I wouldn't like to have hit records, that it would be such a bore and terribly embarrassing to be wealthy. That's bollocks! It's merely that, for whatever reasons, my music career has settled down into a much lower-key groove, where record sales are measured in thousands rather than hundreds of thousands, which has enabled me to lead a much more serene lifestyle.

'When you and I first knew each other, my life was my career. If you said, "How are you?" I'd have told you how my career was doing. I really didn't have much of an existence as a person. If my career went down in the dumper for a time then I was down in the dumper too. I had no sense of self-worth or anything separate from it, whereas now, if the music business packed up on me tomorrow I would still live perfectly happily and find some equally congenial way to pay the rent. That's a compensation.'

It is probably also a compensation of the ageing process, we both agree (but then we would, wouldn't we?) that life is elsewhere than the Album of the Week slot or the front page feature. Success and achievement are ultimately about things other than success and achievement in the career field.

'Richard O'Brien said a very interesting thing,' says Robinson. O'Brien, author of the hugely successful *Rocky Horror Show*, latterly the host of TV's *Crystal Maze* show, and not really noted for much else, 'was asked, are you successful, Richard? "Well," he said, "Success. What is success? We live, we die, we fill in between. Success is a happy life. So, yes, I'm successful."'

Tom Robinson grins. 'I couldn't have put it better myself.'

Chapter thirteen

Oh, Patti

WHILE they might prefer to differ, both Julie Burchill and Gillian G. Gaar concur on the fact that it took the arrival of punk for women to engage in the music industry on an equitable, self-defining basis. Women had, obviously, entered the field in the previous decades, but normally on terms defined by men, or by defining themselves in their difference/resistance to men. With punk, women performers invented themselves from the ground up, even if in the case of Patti Smith, punk's first echt-lesbian, they dressed as boys. History may ultimately pair Smith with Diane Keaton's cute cross-dresser in *Annie Hall*, but her appearance on the sleeve of *Horses* in 1976 was without precedent, and was read as such by feminists, lesbians and gay men. (It is just possible that an earlier generation might have found such symbolism in performers like Joni Mitchell, Dory Previn and Laura Nyro, but I don't believe that they were looking for this.) As Smith's career unfolded, so did the queer pointers; her debts to Rimbaud and Verlaine, her friendship with photographer Robert Mapplethorpe (the Robert in the title of her underground film 'classic', *Robert Having His Nipple Pierced*).

Patti Smith wasn't a dyke, of course — nowadays she's a happily married suburban mom, although she did return to the recording studio in 1988 — but the fact that she was hailed as an iconoclast is a measure of the cramped space that women occupied in music. It would take the arrival of Mathilde Santing for a woman performer to state openly her attraction to her own sex, but punk cleared a space in which women performers could invent themselves as they pleased, and without reference to men. Punk's earliest outbursts relied heavily on bondage clothing and fascist symbolism, including liberal sprinklings of swastikas (although, as Jon Savage points out, these things had and have a claim to polysemy, a variety of interpretations – chiefly, as effects to shock – beyond their crude emblematic fascism), but even Siouxsie Sioux soon disposed of the *Night Porter* chic. Poly Styrene decked herself in 1960s Woolworth camp, the Slits in pre-crustie dreadlocks, cavegirl rags or tutus, bands like The Raincoats and feminist musicians such as Au Pairs' Leslie Wood in the genderless 'grim' look of the late 1970s.

And, again, punk too had its submerged lesbian history, not least in Vi Subversa, of the admirable Poison Girls, who came out as lesbian later on in the career of the band. (It is clear, however, that lesbianism was still a tricky issue even during punk.) It should also be recorded that legendary punk journalist Jane Suck came out as lesbian. She now writes as Jane Solanas, which isn't her real name, either, but a homage to Valerie Solanas, author of the SCUM (Society for Cutting Up Men) Manifesto and the woman who shot Andy Warhol.

The Slits, as the name probably suggests, were probably the wildest of the girl punk groups, although The Raincoats gave them a good run for their money (and FIG, the Feminist Improvising Group, were probably the most radical). Along with colleague Richard Famous, Vi Subversa confronted ageism (both were in their fifties) as well as sexism and homophobia in their work. On albums like *Where's the Pleasure?* they produced politicized popular music which I doubt could be bettered anywhere else (Brecht and Weill excepted), addressing issues as diverse as militarism, Northern Ireland, multinationalism and sex war with passion, humour, irony and unequivocal commitment. Moreover, they did it with those taboo qualities, style and substance, on songs that belied their (mistaken) reputation as anarchist punks.

Punk empowered women performers like, I believe, no movement or fashion before it and gave us, however briefly, the Rock Against Sexism movement (even if my RAS badge did little more than invite a severe earbashing from the Gang of Four's Hugo Burnham for working on the 'sexist' rock paper *Sounds*). As well as ushering in the DIY ethic that saw boys and girls starting their own bands, magazines, labels and even shops, distributors and management agencies, punk also broke moulds around gender and sexuality. Curiously, few (if any) gay men took advantage of this cease-fire – punk happened to coincide with the peak of the disco boom – but scores of women grabbed the opportunity and ran with it. Patti Smith may have been immediately followed by Deborah Harry, whose first British promotion was with the notorious 'Wouldn't you like to rip her to shreds?' poster campaign (and one that may now have taken on an ironic post-modern sheen) but Harry was followed by feminist new wavers like Exene Cervenka of X, Lydia Lunch, Ut and Pulsallama. Later, these would be followed by a wave of newer, even more assertive all-women or women-led bands such as Throwing Muses, Babes in Toyland, L7, Hole, and Belly.

In Britain, Poly Styrene's X-Ray Spex gave birth to her friend Lora Logic's Essential Logic, and women's and pro-feminist bands proliferated. Skipping through a current (1994) issue of the stylish West Coast lesbian magazine *Deneuve*, I discover an unusual album from this era, *We Buy a Hammer for Daddy*, by London's Lemon Kittens, featuring the startling multi-instrumentalist and performer Danielle Dax, at number one in a personal playlist from none other than Gillian G. Gaar (making something of a personal statement therein, I guess). Although heterosexual, Dax and her partner Karl Blake produced a series of startling but accessible experimental albums that dug at the very foundations of sexual identity. Dax went on to launch a solo career, and enjoyed brief fame as the wild-haired creature who crept out of the well in Neil Jordan's *The Company of Wolves*.

In hindsight, it does appear that there were gay men involved in punk and the new wave, although this too is only beginning to emerge (and still leaks out, from sources such as Holly Johnson's autobiography, *A Bone in My Flute*). From the American scene, gay anarchist punks 1,000,000 Dead Cops are one of the few notable names in this first, pre-Homocore movement. In Britain, Gene October of Chelsea was outed when it was revealed that he had appeared in gay pornography magazines. Following the dissolution of The Buzzcocks, guitarist and co-writer Pete Shelley came out as bisexual, which puts a queer spin on such punk classics as 'Spiral Scratch', 'Orgasm Addict' and 'Ever Fallen in Love with

Someone You Shouldn't've?' Shelley went on to record a number of excellent electro-tinged solo projects.

Early punk entourages like the Bromley Contingent found refuge in gay nightclubs such as Louise's and Chaguaramas, and in his autobiography Holly Johnson reports a similar situation in Liverpool. There was also, as in the case of mod, a cross-over between gay and punk fashions in the early days of punk, but again these were the urban elites (of both the gay and new wave movements). Famously, one of the earliest performances by the Sex Pistols was at a party hosted by artist and Alternative Miss World promoter Andrew Logan. But history and memory play funny games with punk. So much has been talked about punk that it seems that one day early in 1976, a Thursday, maybe, everybody suddenly changed overnight into short-haired, pierced and ripped-clothed punks (rather like the fact that if everyone who claims to have been at the early Pistols gigs had really been there, they would have had to hire the Royal Albert Hall). Look back at contemporary photographs of the Sex Pistols at, say, the Nashville, and you notice that apart from the band and friends, 99 per cent of the audience are in flares and have long hair.

Further on into the new wave, Vaughan Toulouse of the ska/dance group Department S, who took their name from a tongue-in-cheek 1960s thriller series starring actor Peter Wyngarde, was quite out about his gayness on the London nightclub scene. Toulouse died of AIDS-related illness in 1991. There is a definite queer subtext to art-house punks Wire, and explicit queer references have appeared in the new wave from The Homosexuals' 'Hearts in Exile' up to The Wolfgang Press's 'Queer'. In America, it is now apparent that there was a queer supertext to The B52's. Bob Mould, of Husker Du and now Sugar, has come out. Others hover in the closet doorway.

There is no suggestion that any members of the Sex Pistols were queer – Sid Vicious dated Nancy Spungen, Cook and Jones are beery lads, and John Lydon is heterosexual enough to have once targeted this writer with a number of homophobic comments. Thanks to Jon Savage, however, we have access to artefacts which put an oddly queer tinge to some of their imagery. Among the wealth of images in Savage's *England's Dreaming*, there are four images of the individual Pistols by Peter Christopherson, taken when Glen Matlock was still in the band. A director of the design agency Hypgnosis (remember all those Pink Floyd sleeves?), and better known for his involvement in noise terrorists Throbbing Gristle, Psychic TV and Coil, Christopherson also designed the controversial body-part installations that graced the windows of the BOY boutique in 1977. These were extremely lifelike bits of a body – a booted foot, part of a hand – that looked as though they had been mutilated, or at least severed, during a fire or explosion. They drew crowds, until the police removed the exhibit from the window. Christopherson, Sleazy to his friends, is quite candid about his interest in SM ritual and gay sex magick, and he also produces photographic works featuring people in carefully posed medical and accident settings (a homoerotic counterpart, perhaps, to the work of American photographer Cindy Sherman). One of these eerie and rather disturbing images, of Christopherson tending a blood-spattered teenager beneath a neon sign that says 'PLAY-LAND', graces the inner sleeve of Throbbing Gristle's *Heathen Earth* album.

Early in 1976, Christopherson photographed the Sex Pistols in similar, if less obvious fashion. Lydon was photographed, smiling, against a wall in a straitjacket; fairly straightforward punk imagery for its time, really. Matlock was posed topless and vulnerable in an institutional or public washroom (the industrial soap and towel dispensers – even though Matlock seems to have his own towel – relocate it away from any domestic setting), the institutional context lending itself to various interpretations. Steve Jones was posed handcuffed and in pyjamas, seated on the floor, surrounded by shadow but with his left hand handcuffed to the arm of someone else (who isn't in pyjamas, but looks like they're in control) out of the frame. Paul Cook was photographed topless in bed, reclining, head to the left but eyes open, two large sores or buboes on his chest, looking for all the world as though he's dying of some medieval plague (and, yes, today they do look a little like Kaposi's sarcoma lesions). The images of Lydon and Matlock might pass for unconventional publicity shots, although there's something both intimate and intrusive about the Matlock shot that makes it look very odd (it could simply be a dressing-room shot, but not when included in this particular quartet of images). The images of Jones and Cook, however, like Cindy Sherman's images of herself in her 'Untitled Film Stills' series, invite you to run little movies of these scenes, filling in the before and after of these enigmatic but loaded images. These little movies are homoerotic narratives in the manner of the late Curt McDowell's autopsy chic movies.

It's unlikely that the Pistols were aware of the full import of Christopherson's work, but that doesn't lessen the homoerotic content of these images. It could hardly be described as incriminating evidence, though, nor is it really meant to be considered as such, but along with Joe Strummer's blowjob from a male admirer captured in the film *Rude Boy*, it throws a few queer curves on people hitherto considered straight.

Chapter fourteen

* Nightclubbing

DANCING, dance music and places where people dance have been central to the lives of queers since queers were first invented. The dancefloor has always been a holy space – you don't need to be a blue-footed booby to know that this is a key mating site – but it is particularly so among men and women attracted to their own sex. It is also a hotly contested space, and some of the things you hear there deserve questioning.

Dance music as it is perceived now – soul, disco, funk, techno and the many mansions of house – is, I believe, the one form of music which, even in its most degraded form, is bound up in something that closely resembles Roland Barthes's notion of *jouissance*, that is, rapture, bliss or transcendence. We could all probably make this claim for other musics; off the top of my head, Wayne Shorter's *Native Dancer*, Scritti Politti's 'The Sweetest Girl' and the Human League's 'Empire State Human' all score high in my *jouissance* top ten. We might also think of musical genres which are equally blissed out; the overt sexuality of salsa brass and montuno piano, say, or the gleeful chatter and bubble of high life or juju. But none of these individual examples or styles can compare with a music whose whole point is both to describe and to induce rapture. As Richard Dyer wrote in his famous essay 'In Defence of Disco', 'This escape from the confines of popular song into ecstasy is very characteristic of disco.'

That disco should need Dyer's defence – and in 1979 it probably did – is itself telling. In the year that Dyer's essay originally appeared in *Gay Left*, a music business wholesaler who commented on changing consumer fashions in music for the trade press told me that in his opinion the influence of the gay market on dance music was waning, a comment which in hindsight might be seen as homophobic wishful thinking, not to mention a little wide of the mark. In the wake of punk and RAR, disco itself was demonized in the minds of pop consumers who considered themselves hip, hence the Death To Disco 'movement' and the burn-ins of Barry White records. To the minds of many, myself included, disco did seem a very insipid music, although there can be no doubt that the Death To Disco movement also identified disco as fag music and was encoded with its own homophobic little message.

As a child I danced to Motown, as a teen to Philly soul, but I drew the line at Brass Construction. And as a gay man who was writing about bands like The Residents and The Pop Group, I fully believed that disco was eating people's brains. (This was prior to the post-modern Enlightenment, when the Pet Shop Boys started applying *auteur* theory to Bobby Orlando.) I found the gay community's emotional investment in disco rather disturbing, and being the only queer on the planet who listened to Can was a position perhaps analogous to Kevin McCarthy's excellent performance in Don Siegel's original *Invasion of the Body Snatchers*.

But then came the 1980s, when we all (at least, those of us who'd forgotten) learned to dance again. Kraftwerk returned from the wilderness with *Computer World*, Kid Creole and the Coconuts toured Britain for the first time, and the *NME*'s Paul Morley and Ian Penman, the Stan and Ollie of po-mo pop crit, threw themselves at the feet of Grace Jones (quite literally, it seems, in the case of Penman). Jones performed her One Man Show at Drury Lane in London, cantering onstage in a gorilla suit, and sent the 99.9 per cent gay audience crazy when she dragged a man onstage and mimed fucking him doggy-fashion. After the austerity of post-punk, which probably reached its nadir with Joy Division's *Closer*, it was hip again to dress up to the nines, take fast drugs and go to clubs like The Lift, where, this time, dub reggae and high life folded in and out of funk and hip-hop. About as far from Brass Construction as you could imagine.

In clubs like The Lift, and its queer promoter Steve

Swindells's later Jungle, I glimpsed the 'romantic/utopian' ambitions that Richard Dyer saw in discos in the late 1970s. Dykes and fairies, breeders and bis, black, brown and pink men and women in any number of tribal outfits, pursuing pleasure and each other in a new church whose ecumenism was truly shocking. I had never seen this at Heaven, but then again I never saw it at the Wag Club or the Haçienda either, and I also have to acknowledge that this sort of thing is not what Heaven is *for*.

A keen Diana Ross fan, Dyer singled out 'Reach Out' and 'Ain't No Mountain High Enough', the latter especially, he says, 'with its lyric's total surrender to love, its heavenly choir and sweeping violins', as key queer disco texts. Funnily enough, Diana Ross was the first name to pop into my mind when contemplating queer disco classics, although I went for 'Love Hangover' and 'Upside Down', the former with its breathtaking syncopated breaks, the latter for its toe-stubbing bassline. What we both seemed to be identifying was a personal notion of musical drama, a pleasurable BPM setting, a *langue d'amour* with which we could identify (maybe), and certain special effects: Dyer was clearly attracted to the melodramatics of those two Ross pieces, and the sentiments declared in those songs; I cleave to the latter two tunes' rhythm and syncopation, which could be read as the text and its punctum, the feature which punctures it, gives it focus and meaning. The lyrics – to Diana Ross or anyone else – may be sweet, cute, romantic or sexy, but as a *langue d'amour* they are illusory and, beyond the immediate effect of the song, disposable.

While I understand the physiological appeal of this music – rhythm, syncopation, melody, narrative, resolution and closure – I still don't understand why gay men in particular identify so violently with this form (lesbians, from what little experience I have of their leisure patterns, seem far more at home dancing to a wider range of musical styles). Lesbians deconstructing Elvis Presley are one thing; queers subscribing to the values of heterosexual (and sometimes homophobic) dance music are another. Richard Dyer's utopian construction sees gay men – and lesbians – finding a commonality in dance music, which becomes a great leveller, transforming differences into likenesses and erasing social barriers, if only for the length of a song/evening/date. This is immensely appealing, but it also overlooks some unpalatable facts about the music, and its makers.

For so queer-related a music, dance music, in any guise you choose to name, is also, disturbingly, the most homophobic music imaginable, with the possible exception of Oi! and individual cretinous rednecks like Guns 'N Roses. Queers may, in the manner of Sue Wise's reading of dead Elvis, be able to appropriate or co-opt aspects of this music, and they may even invent it (wasn't The Bump invented by queers?), but it remains resolutely, and overtly hostile, heterosexual. Even that queer anthem, Sister Sledge's 'We Are Family', was produced by religious fundamentalists. It is here, with dance music, that the tactic Sue Wise used to negotiate her concept of Elvis begins to break down.

Queers continue to dance to and purchase dance music despite its unsavoury politics, just as we continue to consume products made by multinationals we shouldn't support, eat meat and abuse the environment. These are compromises we make in the modern world. But we would do well to contemplate the background against which we dance and buy. We could talk irony and intertextuality until we were blue in the face and dance music would still be about heterosexual hegemony. Worse, when they address the subject of love, which they normally do, the lyrics hymn the sort of relationships, and the sort of politics, that would otherwise be anathema to queers. Worse still, they actively reinforce systems which are, as we read, busily oppressing queers the world over. It may 'only' be a song, but an OutRage! or ACT UP activist dancing in Heaven may well be dancing along to the same value system that might lead to him or her getting beaten up or arrested the next day. I am a former ACT UP activist who has danced to unspeakable heterosexual propaganda, and in Heaven of all places, and I will probably do it again some time, but we should still know what we are dancing to.

Worse, far worse, is the institutionalized homophobia in the dance music field – which we should probably acknowledge as the black music field, although it is increasingly being produced by white musicians and producers, and has, historically, been promoted by white DJs and writers. (We should probably also acknowledge the fact that racism prevented black DJs and writers replacing these white people, although these white people often were and wrote as fervent anti-racists.)

Perhaps the most obvious fact about the black/dance music market is the lack of any single out black pop queer. This is not for the lack of black pop queers – Sylvester proved that, as have other black gay performers like Blackberri, although their self-definition has sometimes resulted in commercial marginalization – but the lack of black pop queers who feel able to come out. This is a difficult subject for a white writer to address, mainly because it involves apportioning blame to sectors of a culture that I as an outsider can never fully understand, and also because black pop queers are probably under certain pressures that I may never fully understand. But certain things are, I believe, obvious.

Many and probably most of us know the names of at least four famous closeted black pop queers. Indeed, if you combine the contents of Gillian G. Gaar's *She's a Rebel* with the contents of Larry Gross's *Contested Closets – the Politics and Ethics of Outing*, you might find that you have ejected some of them from their closets at high speed. Thus does random sampling of information become a do-it-yourself outing kit (but remember, folks, don't try this at home!). In fact, in the meaningless post-modern babble of data in the so-called information superhighway, there may no longer be something that can truly be called a closet any more.

There are two cultural reasons why black pop queers find it difficult and in most cases frankly impossible to come out: family and community pressures, which make it difficult for any black lesbian or gay to come out, and the quite understandable fear that homophobia and racism combined might be enough to destroy a career and perhaps even a life. (Although, although; James Baldwin's ghost tuts at that idea, as does Sylvester's.) Whatever the cause, we seem to know that there are lesbian and homosexual black musicians, but none of them have elected so far to state this publicly.

Sometimes, of course, the pressure to remain in the closet is external; managers and record labels are jealous and even fearful guardians of closets. No famous black pop queer has tested just how powerful these guards are. The failure of an out black pop queer like Sylvester to succeed in chart terms might seem to justify their reasons for remaining closeted, but I'd say that Sylvester's failure to achieve that was the result of homophobia and racism in the music industry, and, ultimately, Sylvester's own decision in the face of that homophobia and racism. When parts of the music industry are run – in Britain – by powerful closeted queers (yes, Britain has its own answer to David Geffen, except this answer to David Geffen doesn't have an answer to Michelangelo Signorile snapping at his heels), it is unlikely that many positive images will be transmitted through the ranks at A&R, marketing or publicity levels. Indeed, there are queers in the music industry who spend much of their time shoring up the closets of famous pop stars.

Unresolved issues around race and sexuality can only increase the pressures on black pop queers. Antipathies towards homosexuals in some sectors of the British and American black communities have flared up in recent years, with black activists calling gay activists racists, and gay activists calling black activists homophobic. There will never be a happy resolution when political differences revolve around involvement in and resistance to fundamentalist religions, Christian or otherwise. While Buju Banton and Shabba Ranks may be particularly vitriolic in their homophobia (just as they are particularly selective in quoting from the Old Testament to bolster their ugly prejudices), they are only the latest in a long line of anti-gay, anti-women and more recently AIDS-scaremongering reggae releases to come out of Jamaica in the last two decades. Bob Marley may have welcomed all and sundry to his punky reggae party, but Rastafarianism enshrines sexism and homophobia as virtues. As recently as April 1994, a small radical black group held a meeting in London at which the audience was told that homosexuals have to be 'destroyed' and that homosexuality is a white sickness that has infected some black men. I can only see these tensions increasing.

Black gay film-maker Isaac Julien, in a filmed confrontation with both Banton and Ranks, opined in closing that it is possible that their homophobia is itself a result of impacted racism. The experience of African-Americans is different even to that of the Central and South Americans who are beginning to outstrip African-Americans in the economy of the United States. As writer Caryl Phillips wrote in his novel, *Higher Ground*, African-Americans didn't land on the Plymouth Rock, 'It landed on them'. This hardly excuses babbling homophobes like Banton or Ranks, but it might explain what causes their irrational hatred of queers.

Women and liberals are beginning to respond, with black women themselves confronting their stereotyping as 'bitches' and 'hos', and rap artists such as The Disposable Heroes of Hiphoprisy have weighed into the fray, recording rap songs that specifically attack homophobia. And, paradoxically, gay men are often at the cutting edge of dance music. If he didn't invent house, then legendary New York DJ Frankie Knuckles was certainly its midwife, DJing nights at New York clubs where up to seven thousand black and hispanic gay men would converge to dance to the hippest sounds likely to be found on Manhattan. The ripples begun by house are still echoing out into the teeming subdivisions of the genre, into ambient and dub. Similarly, as films like Jennie Livingstone's *Paris Is Burning* have shown, vogueing began among working-class black and hispanic queers in New York. Its moves may have been assimilated by mainstream culture, thanks to the attentions of people like Madonna, and to the extent that it is parodied by television comics, but its origins are in the fundamental act of self-invention by poor urban queers. While the trappings may differ, it is also, I believe, related to the rent parties and buffet flats of fifty and sixty years ago. More so than house, which, after all, had nearly half a century of black music history from which it could invent itself, vogueing is an avant-garde movement begun on the street. (It also has an embryonic counterpart in the British Asian–Indian gay community, with the growing trend among some Asian gay men to appropriate Bollywood iconography and cross-dressing in the manner of female Asian film stars to dance to that most radical mixture of dance styles, bhangra.)

Livingstone's film explores the hitherto uncharted territory of the vogueing ball, in particular the Paris ballroom in New York. Groups of streetwise young black and hispanic gays form themselves into groups, or Houses, usually with fashion-related House Of ... names, which become like families, or gangs. The Houses vie to outdo each other's performances at special balls. Individual performers like Willie Ninja may have crossed over into mainstream success, but vogueing as seen on a Madonna video bears little relation to the vogueing at the Paris ballroom. The fashion-plate attitudinizing is similar, but here 'passing', as a woman, as a businessman, even as a member of the armed forces, is vital. This act of reinventing yourself as something else, or of inventing something out of what society sees as 'nothing', is the key. 'Passing' is something that gay men have been taught to distrust, but when life might sometimes resemble a Hubert Selby novel, this fanciful game of bricolage can be one of the few things that make life bearable if you're young, homeless, black or hispanic, and queer, on the streets of New York.

Prior to house, there were (white) gay men at the forefront of dance music on either side of the Atlantic – the late Patrick Cowley, for example, and DJ-turned-producer Ian Levine. It took an article in *The Wire* to inform me that Mark Moore, of S'Express fame, was gay; the number of women he surrounded himself with on the sleeve of S'Express's first album led me to believe he was a heterosexual in too much make-up.

Queers are still emerging in the dance music scene, even if again they are predominantly white. One of the stars of the proliferating ambient scene is DJ-turned-musician (and out queer) Mixmaster Morris, described affectionately by the *Melody Maker* as a 'camp, Jewish ambient space cadet in a holographic suit'. It also predicted that Morris will be 'voted Chap of 1994'. Morris first appeared in London in the early 1980s, trying to set up a variety of experimental one-nighter nightclubs. As The Irresistible Force, the name he records under for the hip indie label Rising High, he became involved in seminal dance group the Shamen's Synergy set-up. He crossed over the turntables to record his cultish first album, *Flying High*, and has worked with leading ambient producer Pete Namlook, particularly on their evocative collaboration, *Dreamfish*. He is wholly out about his sexuality, and has had no negative reactions from colleagues or fans. A great deal of ambient music is poorly-plagiarized Tangerine Dream for people too young to have heard it the first time round (George Santayana's comment about those who forget the past being doomed to repeat it frequently springs to mind, especially when those sequencers start racing). Morris, however, knows his onions. Among the swathes of friends and influences credited on *Flying High*, he thanks 'the god-like genius' of, among others, Sun Ra, Robert Wyatt, Can, Steve Reich, This Heat, Miles Davis, Laurie Anderson, Soft Machine, Edgard Varèse, Harry Partch, Kraftwerk, Henry Cow and John Cage. Quite a few queers in there, and oddly enough his list closely resembles the list of records I would probably attempt to save if my study ever went up in flames.

What all these influences go to produce is an ambient music light years ahead of the usual trance noodlings and bleeps of rave music. It borrows from Latin and African rhythms, jumbles into vocal cut-ups in the manner of Cabaret Voltaire, and on the track 'Hymn' off *Dreamfish* even seems to have a critical word or two to say about Judaeo-Christianity. His *Rising High* also features the most audacious sample I have ever come across. The trick about sampling is to find something sufficiently obscure, preferably deleted. 'Sky High', a 12-minute track off *Rising High*, is a quite shameless steal from an early Kraftwerk tune, 'Ananas Symphonie', off their second album, *Ralf and Florian*. Kraftwerk, who inadvertently helped to launch this whole dance thing back in the 1980s when Afrika Bambaataa hijacked their 'Trans-Europe Express' for the backing track to 'Planet Rock', would probably have been flattered.

The continuing emergence of figures like Mixmaster Morris should not be allowed to obscure the fact, however, that there is still a woeful imbalance between the numbers of out white pop queers and out black pop queers. This is cultural, but it is also commercial. Pop closet doors swing on hinges made of money. Ultimately, it is managers and labels who are keeping in the closet those black artists who have been inadvertently outed by gay historians and critics. From out here, though, it's difficult to tell if they're sheltering in there or being held against their will.

Chapter fifteen

Sisters Doing It for Themselves

IT will come as no surprise that the advice to black performers about what to do with their closet doors is pressed home
firmly on women performers as well. Gary Burton says his friend
k.d. lang was bemused that no other lesbian popular performers
came out after her quite public (if, some would say, a little belated)
coming out, but even that has now been superseded by the equally
public statements by both Janis Ian and Melissa Etheridge.

Considering the near-deafening silence prior to this, broken
only occasionally by performers like Mathilde Santing and Phranc,
the triple coming out of lang, Ian and Etheridge amounts to a queer
landslide. While a number of gay male pop stars have come out
over the last decade, this is quite different to the decisions these
three women have taken and the experiences they have been
through. There is something particular – perhaps its rarity – about
a lesbian pop star coming out that is different, greater and more
dangerous than, say, a comparable male figure coming out, not
least the fact that David Bowie's cynical but effective 'coming out'
two decades ago set a precedent for men, and because countless
men since have made overt or covert play with sexual ambiguity in
a way that few women could or would have dared. Madonna is the
only presumed heterosexual star who has dared to dangle the possibility of covert lesbianism in front of a slavering media.

Even performers like Phranc and Santing caused barely a

ripple beyond the specialist music and queer press, perhaps proving that coming out isn't so difficult for pop queers after all. The mainstream media and, sadly, some queers, were only really interested in the big guns, and such is the cult of celebrity that everyone was still waiting for a Whitney or a Tracey to make that big step. This cult of celebrity, which teaches us to want ever bigger, better and more famous celebrities than the ones we had last week, is a fallacy – perhaps even a phallusy – that diverts us away from the real issues at hand. Celebrities as they are mediated by the daily media are so much Wonderloaf and hamburger meat and aerosol whipped cream, predigested pap pumped out into the media to keep us chewing and sucking on their celebrity status. To get suckered by the celebrity game is to get suckered by the people who make money from it; not just the star, their manager, and their band, but by their record company and publisher, by every ancillary industry involved and by the political parties they support. Every em and en in every column inch is a pound or dollar in some sleazeball's pocket (including, sometimes, mine).

The celebrity game also deliberately confuses fame and talent, often because the former is used to mask a deficiency in the latter. The celebrity game is a ruthless machine, and it is particularly ruthless in its mistreatment of women. And while those who subscribe to it sit and wait for the system to deliver up its sacrificial celebrity queers, another cargo cult that is bound to disappoint, they ignore the ones who are already out. Give me Mathilde and that nice Jewish lesbian with the flat-top any time.

The mainstream media often derides it, even rock journalists who ought to know better, but women have successfully constructed a parallel industry, culture and community for their music when, as they often found, the mainstream industry could or would not deal with it, for reasons of commerciality, or for reasons of bigotry. It is bigger than any other comparable industry, such as jazz, which is essentially an independent industry nowadays, or the new wave, which, with very rare exceptions (Mute's Depeche Mode spring to mind), proves itself too small to hold on to acts as they grow more and more successful (The Smiths, most glaringly). In America, particularly, the women's music industry is a thriving independent.

I am aware of two problems in writing about this topic: (a) I'm a man, and (b) on the topic of the American women's music industry I'm a man writing a few thousand miles away. It is, however, a subject I as a journalist have followed at a certain distance over the years, if only because it seemed to offer a far healthier alternative to the models I found in the mainstream music industry and its alternatives. As a gay man (well, teenager at the time) who sat in a meeting of the Campaign for Homosexual Equality and watched in dismay as the women walked out of the organization (the misogynistic abuse that followed them was a more eloquent expression of their reasons for leaving than anything they could have said) promising to form a women's organization that never materialized, I have long felt that feminists and lesbians have more in common with gay men than they have differences, and that they should form alliances wherever they can. I have also admired the feminist and lesbian movements' ability to develop a non-commercial alternative to the gay ghetto, which, at my cynical worst, might be seen as giving London gays the opportunity to pay Tory heterosexual multi-millionaire Richard Branson a tenner a time for the privilege of getting pissed in a huge cellar under a central London railway terminal.

I also confess that I may have a naive and romanticized image of the American women's music movement, but there are I believe certain facts or phenomena which appear to be true. For one thing, rising out of the folk music culture, it is far more politicized than its British or European counterparts. Performers like Joan Baez (who has come out about her lesbian experiences), Holly Near and Ronnie Gilbert of the Weavers provide a link back to the fine tradition of American resistance and activism that included Woodie Guthrie, the Wobblies (the Industrial Workers of the World) and figures like Emma Goldman. Britain has its own grand tradition of radicalism, of course, even if it is a little thin on the ground these days, but I don't believe it has ever fed into popular culture as in America. Certainly, the British folk scene seems to regard itself more as part of the heritage industry, or possibly an offshoot of the real ale industry. In America, the women's music scene formed links with organizations like NOW (the National Organization of Women, which has no counterpart in Britain) which involved itself in all manner of issues, from health and education, employment and abortion, to the campaign to expose the people who killed anti-nuclear activist Karen Silkwood. It also linked itself to the anti-nuclear movement, and to the (pro-gay, pro-women, pro-abortion) Sandinista government in Nicaragua.

A measure of the size of the American women's movement, apart from the tens of thousands who attend events like the Michigan Women's Music Festival, is the fact that one of the first releases by the (then lesbian-separatist) Washington DC women's music label, Olivia Records, Cris Williamson's *The Changer and the Changed*, released in 1975, eventually sold over a quarter of a million copies. This was, of course, over a period of time, but sales of even a fraction of that could get an album to number one in the British charts in a lean period. The volume of sales on that one album alone give a measure of the size of Olivia's business operation. Comparable releases of such material in Britain would probably measure their pressing runs in single thousands, or even less.

While Olivia has grown to be the biggest women's music label in America, it was by no means the first. The previous year, Wax Records released what is said to be the first out lesbian album, Alix Dobkin's *Lavender Jane Loves Women*. And in 1973, lesbian-to-be Holly Near launched her own Redwood Records, to release her albums of peace and protest music. Near actually came out onstage at the 1976 Michigan Women's Music Festival, when she was in a relationship with another lesbian icon, Meg Christian. As Near explains in her autobiography, *Fire in the Rain ... Singer in the Storm*, she accused an audience of 1,500 lesbians of taking bets on the likelihood that she was a lesbian. 'But you can stop now. I've fallen in love with a woman!'

Near actually started out as an actress. Her most notable role, apart from some episodes of 'The Partridge Family' where she starred alongside 'LA Law's' Susan Dey and David Cassidy, was a part in George Roy Hill's film of Kurt Vonnegut's *Slaughterhouse 5*. By this time, 1971, the twenty-two-year-old Near's life was undergoing dramatic change, anyway. The same year, Near was asked to join FTA, officially known as Free The Army but more commonly known as Fuck The Army, the anti-Vietnam roadshow featuring people like Jane Fonda and Donald Sutherland. This song and dance show culled information from GI newspapers to present a satire of America's policies in Vietnam. It toured America and Indonesia, but the Pentagon never allowed it to visit Vietnam. By the time Near finished touring with FTA, she was writing songs and becoming involved in the peace movement and allied organizations. In 1973, Near launched her own label from the front room of her family home, pressing her family into service as its staff. Her first album, *Hang in There*, a collection of anti-war songs, was released that year, followed by a live album the following year. In 1976 she released *You Can Know All I Am*, the first album explicitly stating her feminist perspective, and since then the label has released more than a dozen of Near's own albums, as well as her collaborations with Ronnie Gilbert, Arlo Guthrie, Pete Seeger, the Chilean band Inti-Illimani, and other signings to Redwood, including the a cappella gospel group, Sweet Honey in the Rock. Her duets with former Weaver Ronnie Gilbert, in concert and on albums like *Singing with You* and *Lifeline*, are a joy, as was her work with the reunited Weavers, captured in the marvellous documentary film *Wasn't That a Time?*

There can be few causes that haven't attracted Near's attention, and it is clear that she has been prepared to put her own safety on the line to support them: the radical film-maker Haskell Wexler, whose film *Medium Cool* famously features footage of its cameraman being hit by a police bullet in a riot, and no stranger to personal danger himself, once pleaded with Near to stay away from a music festival in El Salvador. She went anyway, to show solidarity with Salvadorean musicians, and was in a group who were menaced by soldiers of the American-backed regime.

This has not been altogether easy for Near. She has suffered burnout after too much political work, and at one point told her lover Meg Christian, with whom she had a three-year relationship, that maybe they should get out of 'the women's music rat race'. At one point, she found herself in a conundrum similar to that of Tom Robinson, in a bisexual relationship but defining herself as a lesbian. Trying to peer between the lines of her autobiography, one gets a sense of tension between labels and performers, particularly where the private and personal overlap, although this will occur in any such situation and must have been twice as difficult when these women were inventing something new and risky and perhaps at times fragile and uncertain.

Through their pioneering work in the 1970s and 1980s, women like Near, Christian and Williamson, on labels like Olivia and Redwood, on albums sometimes produced by June Millington, created a stage, metaphorical and quite literal, on which other lesbian and bisexual musicians have begun to appear: Ferron, Two Nice Girls, Michelle Shocked, and now Janis Ian and Melissa Etheridge. Two Nice Girls, however, complained that they didn't want to be 'branded' (their term) as feminists and lesbians, and Shocked, darling of a younger and punkier generation of lesbians, also complained that she felt she was put in a position where she was damned if she did come out, and damned if she didn't. (She subsequently entered a relationship with a man.)

Despite these misgivings, the Michigan Women's Music Festival has to be thanked for this new and unparalleled visibility of lesbian performers. Both Near and Gillian G. Gaar credit it with providing a launching pad for performers like Tracey Chapman and Melissa Etheridge, although Gaar comments that their appearances at the women-only and lesbian-friendly Michigan festival are somehow overlooked in the mainstream media.

The exception to this, of course, is k.d. lang, whose platinum-selling fifth album, *Ingenue*, coincided, more or less, with her coming out to *The Advocate*. There is something suspicious about the 'new fashionability of lesbianism', but that all this should happen together has rocketed lang into a far higher profile than any of her previous albums, performances or media statements.

Rather than Consort, Alberta, lang looks like she should really have come from Cicely, Alaska, home to the collection of cool oddballs who inhabit TV's *Northern Exposure*. (Following their walk-ons for stars like Adam Ant and namechecks for Einstürzende Neubauten – how obscure can they get? – the show ought to offer lang a cameo role seducing 'copter pilot Maggie O'Connell.) Despite her games with cross-dressing and gender confusion in songs, made overt in the cycle of lesbian love songs on *Ingenue*, lang impresses because she seems totally, totally, in control of who she is and what she is doing. Hence the insouciance with which lang can don jokey cowpunk one minute, a wedding dress and veil the next, a three-piece pinstripe man's business suit after that, followed by a shocking pink party frock I swear I once saw on Barbara Cartland. The last time I saw this nerve was on Grace Jones, the cool self-assurance on Laurie Anderson. The appearance of lang on the cover of *Vanity Fair* being 'shaved' by a bikini-clad Cindy Crawford, a spoof of Norman Rockwell Americana shot by Herb Ritts, was her own idea.

Nashville took lang's playful attitude towards tradition as disrespect, and disrespect from the sort of person they would probably prefer to run out of town. But it didn't take too long before some – among them Roy Orbison, Loretta Lynn and Brenda Lee – realized that lang's irreverent attitude could work as paean as well as pastiche. Most, however, resisted her allure, among them the all-powerful radio stations. Lang's career grew regardless, and the (probably homophobic) hostility of the radio stations produced at least one hilarious exposure of redneck bigotry. When a TV ad lang made for People for the Ethical Treatment of Animals (PETA), featuring lang cuddling a cow called Lulu and telling viewers 'Meat stinks', was banned and its content leaked, lang found herself at the centre of a minor media controversy. One beef-interest billboard declared, 'The West Wasn't Won On Salad' (tell that to Castro Street) and somebody sprayed 'Eat Beef Dyke' on a billboard in Consort announcing her link with the town. More seriously, radio stations across the Mid-West announced a boycott of her songs, although as her friends, and gay activists, pointed out, they hadn't actually been playing her records anyway.

It is just as likely that lang's snowballing career was going to roll right over these buffoons, anyway. There is absolutely no surprise that *Ingenue* broke the hearts of a million and one lesbians. (Lesbians? She broke *my* heart.) It opens with a breath of desert air from the location for Donna Deitch's *Desert Hearts*; brushed drums, reversed piano decay noise, steel guitar, Gary Burton's vibes. How much dreamier can a cowgirl expect to get? And that outrageous opening line, those swooning two words, 'Save me!' She might just as well have come round uninvited and fallen into your arms as you opened the front door.

I am no expert on country music – my witting exposure to the genre extends only to the *Nashville* soundtrack, 'Jolene' and

'Ode to Billy Joe', a handful of Ozark Mountain Daredevils albums and some rather obscure recordings by ex-Monkee Mike Naismith – but *Ingenue* has to be one of the most blissed out albums of all time. It straddles camp – clopalong sound effects, *Holiday for Strings* pizzicato, tango devices that might have been borrowed from Astor Piazzolla – and quite ecstatic love balladry, with its ravishing melodies and spine-tingling melismatic harmonies, the latter recalling the work of her fellow Canadian Joni Mitchell. The voice is rarely less than sublime, and the intensity of emotion on a good half of the tracks could get it banned in Boston. In nearly twenty years of fairly constant writing about music, I have never come across anything like it.

Lang's position is virtually unassailable, and likely to build as her career develops further. She has said she is reluctant to take on the role of spokesperson for the gay (seemingly her preferred term) community, but as some commentators have said, she has elevated the issue of coming out to a new level of public awareness. She doesn't appear to have hurt the animal rights movement, either.

Britain has yet to produce a figure to compare to lang, although it has not been without its new generation of good-time, post-feminist women's bands, like the Well-Oiled Sisters. It has also had women pop performers in the mainstream who might have approached the prominence of a k.d. lang, but the difference in climate has kept them and their managers and labels from taking that extra step. One such figure once told me that she just could not take the risk. In an increasingly conservative atmosphere, when the clever and subversive play with gender and persona of a performer like Annie Lennox is considered shocking and avant-garde by a media run by cretins, few pop dykes are going to be prepared to come out to play.

As with the American women's music movement, lesbian and bisexual women performers have created breathing spaces for themselves on the margins of the mainstream, or have walked away from it altogether. Lesbians may not have a high profile on 'Top of the Pops' – until they give Huffty a job, maybe – but they have a high profile in the jazz and new music fields. While not all of the trio have indentified themselves as lesbians, the women's music group Ova built up a reputation both for their own compositions and their workshops with women performers, giving others access to equipment, rehearsal and performance space, and the information to begin to work on their own. Feminist rock groups like the mildly legendary Jam Today, and jazz groups like The Guest Stars and the Lydia D'Ustebyn Orchestra, have all included out lesbian players in their line-up. Singer Maggie Nichols, one of the finest jazz and improvising voices in the country, has identified herself as lesbian for at least a decade. Lesbians were involved in the legendary Feminist Improvising Group of the 1970s, a radical collective of women improvisers who performed household chores as part of their performance – an idea that might have been borrowed from John Cage, although in the context of FIG the musicality of household chores also took on a polemical edge as a statement about women's perceived roles in society. It is also clear that an out and quite vocal lesbian audience has identified its own favourites in the wider music scene. At a local women's music festival gig by singer Carol Grimes and her band supported by superb trombonist Annie Whitehead leading a band that featured the dazzling pianist Jasper van't Hof, we found ourselves in a predominantly lesbian audience, more, in fact, than you could shake a stick at (which would, in any case, probably be inadvisable), and certainly more than I thought lived in south-east London.

One man's attempt to present a roundup of recent lesbian music history is bound to be deficient, although not, I believe, beyond the remit of a male writer who hopes he has some awareness of feminist and lesbian issues. I doubt, however, that a lesbian writer would find a great deal more material, particularly in the mainstream. In a world where, at Laurie Anderson's last computation, on 'Beautiful Red Dress' on her *Strange Angels* album, for every dollar a man makes, a woman only makes 63 cents, and she made only 62 cents fifty years ago, meaning that it'll be the year 3888 before she makes a buck, that still puts women, and lesbians in particular, at the back of the bus.

Chapter sixteen

Like Boy George Never Happened

ONE afternoon in February 1985, Jimmy Somerville arrived at the offices of a magazine I worked on in Covent Garden in London, accompanied by his manager, Anthony Kowalski. We had been friends ever since Bronski Beat contacted the magazine, asking us to review them. He challenged a colleague and me to guess where he had just been. We proffered a variety of increasingly outrageous suggestions, starting with Joe Allen's and ending up with either the clap clinic or prison. Close, was his reply.

He had in fact just been released and fined after pleading guilty at nearby Bow Street magistrates' court on charges of gross indecency with another man. He had been arrested having safe sex with another guy in a secluded part of Hyde Park late at night. If he had been apprehended with a member of the opposite sex, the cops would probably have told them to clear off home. Because he and his partner were both male, it became worthy of arrest, and arraignment, and probably ended up contributing to the statistics the cops use to support their fanciful statements about the war against crime.

This victimless crime (and I really don't even think it can count as a crime), something the vast majority of people, hetero, homo or bi, have done in differing circumstances at some time in their lives, cost Somerville a few hundred quid in fines (he paid his partner-in-crime's fines) plus costs, although it cost Somerville himself rather more. The arrest, and ensuing publicity, seemed to put doubts on an upcoming American tour, including the possibility that Somerville might be refused a work visa. Somerville disappeared off to Paris to wait for the dust to settle, and by the time he returned to London Bronski Beat, at least this incarnation of it, had split up.

The band had barely been in the public eye for a year. An embryonic version had been seen in the award-winning documentary *Framed Youth – Revolt of the Teenage Perverts*. They began playing a few live gigs in clubs like the original Fridge in Brixton, then done out all in white with white camouflage netting to suggest the interior of a freezer compartment. They reminded me a little of the original Human League, except this lot were queer and drawing on disco influences as well as Kraftwerk and glam-rock beat. Yet this wasn't the sort of Hi-NRG that people were dancing to in clubs; in fact, I suspected that Bronski Beat wouldn't go down too well in Heaven. They wore T-shirts and jeans on stage, came from the sticks, had punky-lefty political attitude and sang about how it felt to be queer in the 1980s in Margaret Thatcher's Britain. The baby Jesus had answered my prayers.

Music had gone through a rather strange period in the early 1980s. In the wake of punk and the assimilation of new wave, pop was getting up to its old tricks again. People were dressing up and going to nightclubs. Cocaine became the in drug. Distressingly, guitar heroics were making a comeback, particularly in the ascendance of U2. Pop was becoming safe and harmless again, and the biggest icon of the era, gender-bender Boy George, the not-queer queer you could take to tea with your mum, was about as threatening as Big Bird from *Sesame Street*.

And I was very very tired of queer pop groups who either lied through their teeth or put on the Oscar Wilde/Jean Genet/John Rechy act. David Bowie had done that fifteen years ago. The first Smiths album had queer written all over it, although a rather sickly, clammy inversion of it. (Morrissey got his own back by telling the *Melody Maker*, in his New Year predictions for 1985, that I would 'learn English'.) So did Soft Cell, and 'Say Hello, Wave Goodbye' was a stunning tune, but Marc Almond insisted on encoding the queerness in a hammy drag-act, part Garland, part Piaf, part Ida Lupino in the final reels of *High Sierra*. (Marc got his own back, in a very literary and genuinely funny way, by sending me a porn mag, some raw liver, a small pack of tissues and a note that said I seemed to have a few problems. I responded with a Gay Vegetarians badge, a copy of *With Downcast Gays* and a still of Rita Moreno dancing in *West Side Story*.) And Boy George, deflecting any questions about homosexuality or bisexuality, simply said he preferred a nice cup of tea to sex.

I had and have nothing against camp, but there are times like these when it is simply inappropriate and even dishonest. Had I really been marching for gay pride since the beginning of the 1970s so that in the mid-1980s queer pop stars could still skulk around using code, secret handwriting, closet semaphore and fairy freemason handshakes? At a time when gay men were beginning to die in their thousands, did we really want to perpetuate outdated marginal images which only enabled homophobes to disempower queers even more? Reclaim the dignity of the queens who started the Stonewall riots by all means, but don't let them be hijacked by right-wing pop ideologues like Julie Burchill, whose comment that she prefers her queens in sequins and satin is in fact code for the fact that she would probably prefer 'her' queens in body bags.

Worse still, it isn't only bigots like Burchill who find it convenient to marginalize queers in some glittery decadent netherworld. Even seemingly liberal educated middle-class commentators prefer their pooves exotically strange and therefore containable. When they're not out-and-out homophobes, heterosexual critics love exotic queers; they're somehow more authentic, funky, ethnic, even. At the very least, they're certainly entertaining. The legendary urban myth about Marc Almond's visit to a hospital casualty department – to have his stomach pumped because he swallowed 'too much' semen at an orgy! – is an anatomically bizarre heterosexual fairy tale, but it has attained true mythic status among some straight critics, who have even taken to referring to it in shorthand, perhaps to signify just how hip they are. (On a more surreal note, the American writer Boze Hadleigh applied this myth to Rod Stewart. I wouldn't want to be in Boze's cuban heels when Stewart's lawyers discover this.)

The hostility that greeted the first Bronski Beat album confirmed this. Queers from the Planet Fairy were fine; queers who started taking on the bodies of Earthlings, like the plotline in every paranoid 1950s Sci-fi movie, were not. Forcing critics to deal with their homosexuality on a personal, everyday level, rather than as a literary conceit, a fashion statement, a zoological specimen or – that sub-Baudrillardian *Face* favourite – an anthropological case study, provoked some very Freudian reactions from some critics. One *NME* critic, in a review that seemed to be undercut by an actual fear of homosexuals, snapped 'I don't want to know what they do with the lights off.' (They did, however, print my letter explaining that it's usually more fun with the lights *on*.) In effect, what the Bronskis were saying, for the first time ever, was 'We're here, we're queer, get used to it'.

What was all the more admirable about the Bronskis, however, was that while the boys from the pop press were found unzipped and with their prejudices hanging out, shoppers in Our Price and Woolworth and Virgin fell in love with the band. The chart success of 'Smalltown Boy', the queer 'She's Leaving Home', can be attributed in part to a large gay following – who were, in effect, buying their first real queer record ever – but what took it up the charts was the general public's response to the voice, the melody, the rhythm and the lyric. Once again, the old saw about liking one if you met one endeared these three left-wing queer squatters to a nation of young female *Top of the Pops* watchers and their families (well, okay, their mums). Furthermore, sometime *Sun* columnist Jonathan King absolutely loathed them. They had to be doing something right.

Unfortunately, the age-old problems of money, power, record company control and direction set about the Bronskis with undue haste and ferocity. While members Steve Bronski and Larry Steinbachek were happy, or at least pragmatic, about compromises with the label (its insistence, for example, that the age of consent statistics from the British release be excised from the sleeve of the American release), Somerville suddenly found himself in a place his politics told him he didn't want to be. Uncomfortable and perhaps even unable to cope with fame, business and money, and neither well-suited nor willing to play record company politics, he wanted out. The American tour was duly cancelled, and a legal statement by the band hastily prepared.

They managed to get through the split without too much rancour, and speaking in the week of the break-up both sides of the split told me that they wanted to make the transition as amicable as possible. Looking back, however, there does appear to have been some older history to the split: Somerville was already working on a new project, a collaboration with Richard Coles that would become The Communards, the week of the split.

The Bronskis went on to reform, but never achieved the level of success, commercial or critical, of their first incarnation. Somerville and Coles's Communards, named after the revolutionaries who formed the Paris Commune in the French Revolution, had two hit albums and a string of hit singles, including their debut, 'You Are My World'. With singer Sarah Jane Morris, conscripted from the marvellous Brecht/Weill big band Happy End, the Communards also involved themselves in a number of causes, among them the Red Wedge campaign to lure younger voters back to the Labour Party. But disenchantment set in again, perhaps for Coles as well as Somerville, for Coles was contemplating converting to the Roman Catholic faith, and Somerville went solo, releasing *Read My Lips*, followed in 1990 by a successful singles compilation. Somerville's political commitment rarely wavered. He did admit, once, and in passing, that at times he wondered if he should have been so upfront about his sexuality and politics – it had led to brawls with other pop stars, abuse and threats on the street, even, when he was still living in a squat in south London, an attack on the flat by skinheads – but his attitude was unwavering when he supported causes like Red Wedge. And as *Read My Lips* might suggest, after going solo Somerville became a tireless supporter of ACT UP, buying ACT UP London a phone line and answerphone, helping out with random bills, putting himself on the frontline at ACT UP actions, and sitting through endless fractious and often confrontational meetings at the London Lesbian and Gay Centre.

In the immediate aftermath of the Bronski split, after so brief a career (which might have fitted rock mythology but didn't serve either their or our agendas) it seemed that, with a year or more to wait for any further output from either side, as far as queer pop fans were concerned, it was back in the closet with Mozza and Big Bird. However, this was to be overturned in a matter of months with the arrival of another lippy working-class queen with attitude, Holly (né Billy) Johnson, his butch-looking friend Paul Rutherford, and three heterosexual musicians, Brian Nash, Mark O'Toole and Peter Gill, who, if Johnson's autobiography is to be fully believed, appear on Frankie Goes to Hollywood's most famous song only in the form of a splashing noise they all made jumping into a swimming pool which was sampled by producer Trevor Horn and deployed as an effect on the various mixes of 'Relax'.

As *A Bone in My Flute must* have been read by a libel lawyer, Holly's side of the story must be fairly true, or quite near the mark. His book might still, however, be teensily creative with certain nuances of fact. The notoriety of some of the industry figures he encountered is unquestionable, although Holly's attempts to paint himself and partner Wolfgang as white as the driven snow are at best faux-naif, at worst as disingenuous as Belle Poitrine's cult memoirs, *Little Me*.

I met Holly-qua-Frankie twice, once on the way up, once on the way west, and both times with a tape recorder. Our first interview, which started at the Columbia Hotel, then a popular rock biz dormitory for out-of-town artists, was in the period of the release, and prompt banning by Radio One, of 'Relax'. Frankie had done a PA in London, dressed in their leather finery, throwing a blow-up sex doll around to a taped backing track, and their launch looked like it could be fun. I was on nodding terms with Paul Morley, the journalist who had launched their label with Trevor Horn, whom I had met (and distrusted) when he jumped ships from the execrable Buggles to join, ahem, Yes. I even knew the Futurist manifesto by Filippo Tommaso Marinetti, *Zang Tumb Tumb*, from which Morley borrowed the label ZTT's name: curiously, both he and Holly consistently misspelled Marinetti; Morley insisting it was Zang Tuum Tumb, Holly that it was Zaang Tuum Tumb (so at least they had *one* thing in common). Knowing his interest in Barthes and similar writers, I suspected that Morley hoped ZTT/Frankie would be another pop Situationist whirl in the manner of Malcolm McLaren and the Pistols. Well, he got some of it right.

Perhaps expecting a heterosexual interviewer, or maybe just hoping to liven up the copy, Holly first spent some time telling me about the night before, when he'd been at a club and this gorgeous guy had spent an age dialling his tits. I must have said something that passed muster as queer, because we then went shopping: like the saying goes, when the going gets tough, the tough go shopping. We took a taxi to the King's Road, where Holly put a down payment on a Claude Montana jacket that cost more than I earned in a month, and where he bought a plain white T-shirt for more than I had, up till then, ever paid for any single item of clothing. But then no one ever accused me of being a clothes-horse.

This was hardly a setting in which to conduct an interview, although as we window-shopped it became apparent that Johnson was a likeable, sharp-witted, clever and funny person who knew what he wanted out of life. There was no doubt, however, that Johnson was enjoying the controversy around FGTH, and feeding it himself.

The controversy finally died down and Frankie hit the road. Despite the arguments over how much of it was taped and who was playing and singing what, the show, which was what Frankie were about, was dazzling. A later live debut that was also surrounded with accusations of media hype, the disastrous and embarrassing Royal Albert Hall concert by the appalling Sigue Sigue Sputnik, with 'discreet' queer Martin Degville on vocals, was little more than a joke compared to Frankie. I took a friend's daughter to one of the Hammersmith Odeon shows, and by chance she was hauled out of the audience by Johnson to dance with him on stage. I told him how much we enjoyed the show the next time I saw him.

The next time we met was in slightly different circumstances. The Frankie campaign was in disarray, and, as his book now reveals, Johnson was in an intolerably isolated position with the band, the label and its henchmen. (Morley earns barely a handful of mentions in the book, but in one of them Johnson half-jokingly wishes Paul and his wife, Propaganda's Claudia Brucken, dead under the wheels of a car in an accident staged for a Frankie video.) This time, Holly, with partner Wolfgang in attendance, was backpedalling furiously over the controversy, insisting that the 'Relax' lyric was a harmless and sexless ditty he had made up to hum as he walked to the rehearsal studio (the book version, except I don't remember the walk to the studio being in the book). I drew

down the ire of Wolfgang, who took exception to the pink triangle
badge that lived on a particular jacket of mine in those days. I wore
the badge for political reasons, and would not have removed it even
if I'd been warned that Holly Johnson had a German boyfriend
who insisted on sitting in on interviews. Wolfgang sniffed dismis-
sively that I was 'one of those type of gays', which, from reading
Johnson's book, seems to mean that I wasn't a British Airways
steward with a Bee Gees hairdo. The triangle had caused a few
problems before; it appeared to terrify Green Gartside of Scritti
Politti, inspired the aforementioned attack from John Lydon, and
seemed to amuse members of The Residents' entourage, perhaps
because I had been on tour with them in Germany for three days
before they reminded me that I was wearing it. It seemed ironic, and
in hindsight rather sad, that it should cause the greatest fuss with a
pair of queers.

This interview proved little better than our first; Johnson
was being painstakingly diplomatic, if Wolfgang wasn't in the
driving seat of whatever Johnson said he was definitely navigating,
ZTT, who had their representative there, were trying to tamp down
the controversy, and, unfortunately for Wolfgang, he was about to
become the queer answer to Linda McCartney, wrongly blamed for
all the ills that beset the more famous partner's band.

Frankie, and come to that ZTT, began to unravel in a series
of increasingly acrimonious public and private disputes between
Johnson, the rest of the band, ZTT and its directors. The factual
parts of Johnson's book outline a particularly unfair business contract between label and band, which effectively penalized the group
the more successful they became, while lining the pockets of those
who ran the label and its subsidiaries. It is a particularly chastening
read for anyone who has ever aspired to pop stardom, and for
anyone who has ever been suckered by the myth of pop stardom:
throughout Frankie's greatest days, Holly Johnson was earning
forty quid a week.

He eventually earned a lot more, of course, and made pop
history when he took ZTT to court to dispute the contract they had
him in and won. By that time, he had walked out on Frankie, and
launched a successful solo career. But already Johnson's priorities
were undergoing rapid change. As his autobiography explains, he

had feared for some time that persistent minor illnesses and infections might be HIV and could presage what used to be called conversion to ARC, AIDS-related complex. A biopsy of a lump on his stomach in 1991 proved it to be Kaposi's sarcoma, which spells AIDS. Johnson wrote his book to pre-empt any scuzzy faked autobiographies, unofficial biographies and in-his-own-words cut-and-paste jobs. He also agreed to talk to freelance journalist Alan Jackson for an interview for *The Times* in which Johnson would discuss his AIDS diagnosis. A whizz-kid hack at Jonathan King's favourite paper, the *Sun*, hacked into *The Times* features files, found the Johnson story in a computer file, and probably won him/herself either a bonus, rise or better job when the *Sun* ran with its 'Holly Dying Of AIDS' cover. Johnson sued them, too, and won. He is currently as healthy as someone living with HIV and Kaposi's sarcoma can be.

The world turns. When the dust settled after Frankie bit the dust, it became apparent that there was little more that pop queers could do now, although the Frankie media spectacle seemed, if anything, to shore up a few well-known closet doors. Frankie seemed to make male homosexuality in pop a commonplace, at least as far as the media were concerned, although it had long been evident that, in or out, the media were prepared to negotiate this topic only on their terms. But at last unabashedly queer or queer-led pop groups, from A Blue Mercedes to indie darlings Kitchens of Distinction, were beginning to appear.

Chapter seventeen

Queer Noises

IF this book has tended at times to concentrate on areas that some might consider avant-garde, it is not simply because of the author's (quite unashamed) preference for queer noise, but because the avant-garde, as this book has I hope shown, is often driven by queers. The avant-garde, in whatever form it takes, is a brave stab at guessing the future, or exploring alternatives, even if the current avant-garde, post-modernism, seems to be camping around with pick'n'mix retro.

In the past decade, I have – often unwittingly – stumbled upon queers in the breaking wave of the avant-garde. One sunny Saturday afternoon early in the 1980s, a colleague and I found ourselves wandering the streets south of Blackfriars Bridge, on a caper that was straight out of Thomas Pynchon. A band who had given us a tape of their music, crashing industrial gamelan music battered out of steel springs, oil drums, sheets of metal, vast tanks, bits of machinery, using hammers, drills and buzzsaws, had invited us to one of their performances. The precise address of the concert had to be kept secret. They hired industrial premises – railway arches, warehouses, industrial depots – under the guise of anonymous charities, in case the owners and the authorities got wind of what they intended to do in, and sometimes with, this property.

We were told to keep an eye out for their initials – TD, for Test Dept, a collective from New Cross in south London which I later learned had a number of gay men among its members – and follow the arrows sprayed next to them. We finally found the signs sprayed on the side of a building, and set off, ending up at the gates to a disused industrial workshop where a hundred or so people who wouldn't normally be found in such a setting were hanging about, looking shifty.

It was probably the only concert I've attended where I wondered if I was going to die. Test Dept were (and remain) stunning, breathtakingly noisy and quite terrifying, in a way that neither of their nearest counterparts, Berlin's Einstürzende Neubauten and London's Bow Gamelan Ensemble, have ever been. As they drummed up metal thunder on an adventure playground's worth of industrial detritus, violent electronic noise was bled into the mix and grainy Russian revolutionary films were projected on to band and stage. The audience, most of whom had obviously seen Test Dept before, knew enough to stay well away from the stage. The smell of oil was everywhere, and when they began applying cutting machinery to their instruments, producing volcanic spurts of sparks 20 feet across, people stubbed out cigarettes and backed towards the one tiny door.

We got out, of course, scared, thrilled, awestruck. It obviously had its precedents, in 1960s performance art, in Jean Tinguely's self-destructive motorized sculptures, and in the machine and factory music of the Italian Futurists, although where the Futurists pandered to Fascism Test Dept's heroes were the Russian Constructivists. But it had absolutely no precedent in the field of popular music.

That was probably the last time Test Dept did an unofficial concert like that. The next one I tried to attend, in a railway arch nearby, was stopped by the police, who arrived after a tip-off (possibly from the railway board, suspicious of the bogus charity event it had been booked for) and promptly arrested the musicians. Later performances tended to be more official: commandeering the whole of Cannon Street station for a performance that was almost disrupted by drunken Nazi skinheads; transforming a West London industrial depot into a huge clanking machine filled with moving sculptures, dancers and musicians; and staging a vast industrial May Day event in a Clyde shipyard. Most interviews with Test Dept were political, and they certainly never discussed sexuality with me. By the time I heard of a gay involvement in the group, its core had relocated to Glasgow. They said they first began making music just for the sheer hell of beating shit out of an inanimate object, but their work took on a powerful political edge, identified with the left but in fact more likely anarchist; in *Beating the Retreat*, as one of their albums was called, they may have been drumming for an end to Thatcherism, but they were also drumming to lament the demise of British industry.

About the same time that Test Dept were risking life and limb in every performance, two unholy terrors were hatching explicitly queer outrages on the periphery of the mainstream. Peter Christopherson, the man responsible for the BOY window displays and the homoerotic photographs of the early Pistols, is no stranger to controversy. As a member of Throbbing Gristle, the 1970s art/noise guerrilla squad, he had sometimes performed concerts which, like a particularly notorious concert at London's Filmmakers' Co-op, dissolved into riots. TG did not actually incite the riots themselves – this began as an attack on the band from a gang of Slits and Clash roadies – although some aspects of their performances, films that appeared to show scenes of castration, frightening electronic discord (which they dubbed Music from the Death Factory), iconography that could be mistaken as crypto-fascist, songs that took their titles from the gas used in the Nazi death camps ('Zyklon B Zombie') or that catalogue a medical black museum of horrors, were frequently provocative. His partner, Genesis P. Orridge, a fine arts graduate and art historian who had been involved in the Fluxus movement in Britain, was once put on trial at the Old Bailey for sending 'obscene' material through the post, but a coach party of artists and writers gave evidence in his defence and Genesis was acquitted. With his TG collaborator, sometime stripper and performance artist Cosey Fanny Tutti, he also staged an exhibit of used tampons at the ICA in London. The tabloids had a field day.

In 1981, Throbbing Gristle disbanded; black-edged postcards sent to the media announced 'The Mission Has Been Terminated', and added that following the termination of the project their label, Industrial Records, would no longer be accepting mail orders for their product.

Orridge and Christopherson resurfaced the following year as Psychic TV, and with a spanking new album which ditched the primitive noise terrorism of TG for clever sampled sounds recorded on a revolutionary new 'Holophonic' system. One of the highlights of this project, first heard on their album *Force the Hand of Chance*, was the sound of being buried alive. Orridge and Christopherson had also plunged into the culture of body piercing; during an interview they proudly showed me their brand new Prince Albert penis rings, among other things, which they said had been painless to insert and which immensely increased sexual pleasure. I took their word on that one.

Christopherson left Psychic TV shortly after its foundation, and with his partner John Balance formed Coil, whose 1984 debut recording, 'How to Destroy Angels', a wash of temple gongs and bells, was subtitled 'ritual music for the accumulation of male sexual energy', and they weren't joking. Their distributors, Rough Trade, gave them a hard time about the male exclusivity of the project, but the self-styled sex magick initiates stuck to their guns. With subsequent albums, such as *Scatology* (they weren't joking there, either) and *Horse Rotovator*, Coil outdid Psychic TV with a sophisticated and eclectic sound that saw no difficulty in moving from medieval fanfares one minute to Lalo-Schifrin-style brass arrangements the next, and straddling sampled funk to eerie electronic landscapes.

They ran into trouble in 1985 with their cover of Soft Cell's 'Tainted Love', particularly with the sleeve note that announced that profits from the record would go to the Terrence Higgins Trust. In America, in particular, where their work would have been relatively unknown and their motives open to misinterpretation, they were called sick and evil. Some stores boycotted the release, and gay record store owners wrote to denounce them. Their cover of their friend Marc Almond's song was, in fact, a quite heartfelt, if controversial, response to the AIDS crisis, a powerfully romantic reading of the original, refuting the demonization of homosexuality in the media. This was at the time when HIV was still known as HTLV-3, when epidemiology was barely beginning to comprehend the scope of the epidemic, and when doctors and scientists I had interviewed in London admitted that they were still flailing around in the dark. Little surprise that Christopherson and Balance – two very sweet men who live together, in fact, but who, like writers Kathy Acker and William Burroughs, are sometimes mistaken for the content of their work – were misread. Coil remain one of the most innovative units working anywhere in popular music in this period.

Until the early 1990s, I was unaware that since the late 1970s I had been carrying a queer combo around in my All-Time Top 10 Desert Island Discs. The disc in question is *Half-Mute*, the debut album by San Francisco's Tuxedomoon, released in 1979 on The Residents' record label, Ralph. Their backgrounds included the conservatoire, jazz club, disco, punk dive and tea dance. They were/ are an 'art' band, but I would place them above and beyond any art band you care to name: Talking Heads, King Crimson, Shriekback, Devo, Pere Ubu, Frank Zappa, even The Residents. On that one album, Tuxedomoon summoned up the blue ache of Mingus and Parker, the hypnotic undertow of beat pop, the keening of gypsy violins, the alienated twitch of punk, the pulse of electro, and any number of levels of dizzying camp, which managed both to be post-modern at a time when the term was still relegated to architectural theory and still say something new.

I met Tuxedomoon in London in 1979, when they passed through en route for Europe, fleeing, they said, Ronald Reagan's America. Their sensibilities are probably more European, anyway, even if some of their influences are American jazz and cinema music. They settled in Brussels, and produced a series of albums, including 1984's excellent *Holy Wars*, as well as a number of solo albums.

Tuxedomoon eventually became an umbrella name for a grouping of like-minded musicians who collaborate on an oc-casional basis. Singer Winston Tong returned to San Francisco, where he recorded a European club hit, 'Theoretical China', and later toured with a cycle of Ellington songs recast in an avant-garde setting (an interesting, if accidental, queer connection there). The two remaining core members, violinist Blaine Reininger and saxo-phonist/singer Steven Brown, remained in Brussels.

I met Reininger and Brown in London in 1990, when they were touring with a contemporary dance group. Updating each other on several years of missed history, I explained that I had become involved in ACT UP London. Out of the blue, Brown replied that he was a member of ACT UP Brussels. 'Funny we never knew that we were both gay,' Brown wrote, this time from Mexico, having moved there in 1993. This is one of the vicissitudes of journalism: unless it is stated, or unless the interviewer asks almost automatically, it is silently assumed that the interviewee is hetero-sexual (time, perhaps, to don those 'How dare you ...' badges again). 'I always thought that everyone in SF knew Tuxedomoon was a gay band,' the band's one heterosexual, Reininger, wrote from Brussels. 'Winston, Steven, that is. Not I.' What can I say? No one told *me*.

Other queers are easier to spot. British composer Steve Martland makes no bones about his sexuality, dressing to conduct his classical ensemble in Docs, Levis and white T-shirt, clothing which, with his cropped hair, accentuates his muscle-builder frame. While this look is part of a fitness regime, it also gives Martland the appearance of someone who is off to the London Apprentice as soon as he can drop his baton.

Martland graduated from Liverpool University and studied composition under composer Alexander Goehr at Cambridge. He then moved to the Netherlands, to work with the acclaimed and, to some, notorious Dutch minimalist Louis Andriessen. Andriessen differs from American minimalists like Glass and Reich in the sever-ity and rigour of his work. Martland heard Andriessen play in Liverpool with his band, Hoketus, and decided that was what he wanted to write.

Andriessen's influence surfaced on the extraordinary *Babi Yar*, Martland's first album, released in Britain by Factory Records, and also on the accompanying *Drill*, a muscular workout for twinned grand pianos. Martland gained especial note with his sub-sequent *Crossing the Border*, a virtuoso 24-minute piece for twenty-six very fit and nimble string players which, while some critics saw echoes of anything from Britten and Tippett to Gorecki, astounded with its compositional power.

Martland has collaborated with Test Dept, the now-defunct Loose Tubes big band (formed by a queer – mine!), singer and sometime Communard Sarah Jane Morris, for whom he wrote the song cycle *Glad Day*, and the Dutch street orchestra, De Volhard-ing. He and writer Stevan Keane have collaborated on a number of words and music pieces, reflecting Martland's uncompromising (if sometimes simplistic) left-wing politics, and this is a theme that runs through his work in film, theatre and television. Oddly, though, given his upfront (and perhaps even fuck-off) attitude about his sexuality, it is the one thing that the media elides in its adulatory coverage of Martland's fast-track career at the front line of contemporary composition.

If this queer avant-garde seems decidedly masculine, I can only apologize that I have failed to uncover any lesbians in this sector. I must, however, pay tribute to a phenomenal woman performer, the one and only Diamanda Galas. What this singer, composer and performer has done with her career, virtually devoting it to an ever-evolving vocal performance piece commenting on the AIDS crisis, is quite extraordinary.

I first met Galas in 1982, before the term AIDS had even been coined by American doctors. She was in Britain to perform the pieces off her debut album, *The Litanies of Satan*, which had been released by the extremely trendy Y Records, home to the legendary Pop Group, Shriekback and, briefly, our friend Sun Ra. *Litanies of Satan*, a howling experimental recital of the Baudelaire poem, was enough to wake the ghost of Cathy Berberian. It was twinned with the marvellously titled 'Wild Women with Steak Knives', whose title alone was enough to inspire thoughts of vagina dentata among heterosexual men. Valerie Solanas's SCUM Manifesto had, if memory serves, merely suggested implements that were sufficiently sharp. A decade before Lorena Bobbitt, Galas was specifying domestic utensils, things that could be grabbed off restaurant tables. The title suggested the wives of Stepford getting their own back using a few ideas borrowed from Burroughs's wild boys. In concert, Galas performed like a woman possessed, with a terrifying physical and vocal power. Cathy Berberian may have pushed out the limits of what the contemporary vocal voice could do, but she hadn't begun to approach the phenomenal intensity and vision of a performer like Galas.

Shortly afterwards, Galas began losing friends, and even family (a brother) to the AIDS epidemic. In 1986, she recorded the first in a trilogy of albums addressing themselves to the AIDS crisis, using biblical texts, poetry by Baudelaire and De Nerval, negro spirituals and her own raging plague poetry denouncing the authorities who allowed the epidemic to develop and spread unchecked. The searing, nerve-shredding anger of Galas's work is a monstrous and beautiful thing to behold. The first album, *The Divine Punishment*, was followed by *Saint of the Pit* and then *You Must Be Sure of the Devil*, the cover of which featured Galas, a statuesque Greek-American woman here resembling a Carmen Saura diva, wielding a pistol, and the libretto was a hellfire tract on AIDS hypocrisy that would give Larry Kramer the vapours. Words fail the extraordinary power of Galas's work. Listening through her trilogy, and the subsequent *Plague Mass*, you get the sense that this woman will pursue the men and women responsible for letting AIDS blossom on Earth into the deepest depths of Dante's Inferno in order to make them pay. Little surprise that Galas has built a reputation stretching from the shipyards of Gdansk, where *The Divine Punishment* was premièred, to the opera houses of America, where she learned her art before defecting into new music.

A different sort of queer avant-garde has been rumbling louder and louder since the late 1980s, and finally went public in recent years with America's Homocult/Homocore wave, and in Britain first with the dyke contingent in Riot Girrl and then with Queercore. I first caught a hint of it with the appearance of in-your-face queer post-punks Tongue Man, whose leader Spud Jones died in April 1994 (of cancer, not, as some assumed, of AIDS-related illness). Jones seemed to have decided that his mission on Earth was as an irritant to the gay scene's 'disco bunny' culture, which he despised as bourgeois and self-deluding. He also had a few pithy things to say about Jimmy Somerville, not least that he didn't mind Jimmy's work but why did it always sound like he was hearing from Gloria Estefan rather than Jimmy?

Spud Jones didn't make many friends in the gay media. One editor dismissed his work as the sort of thing someone could put together at home with tapes, which is rather like saying 'Crosstown Traffic' is the sort of thing you get when you give a black man a guitar. Some aspects of Tongue Man are silly, not least Jones's cod-American accent, his fondness for Burroughs and Beat poetry shock tactics, but Jones's work verged on sick genius. His inspired and demented rants, and the psychotic thwack of Tongue Man's music, were hot-wired direct into the spirit of bands like The Fall, Captain

Beefheart, the Velvets and, I'm sorry but I have to say it, classic Can. Using live instrumentation or machines, Tongue Man wielded an elemental wallop that suggested a nightmarish queer collaboration between Tom Waits and Deutsche Americanische Freundschaft. It is hardly surprising that Tongue Man scared faint-hearted gay critics, or that Jones's message to his disco bunny detractors should be 'eat shit girls!'

Spud Jones was edited out of some roundups of Queercore, but there can be no doubt that Tongue Man predated this latterday queer punk irruption. In America, the new queer punk was based around labels like San Francisco's Outpunk, responsible for releases by key Queercore band Pansy Division, who already have a following in Britain. The flames were fanned by fanzines like *Homocore* and Bruce La Bruce's *JD's*, which carried features on such figures as the legendary Vaginal Creme Davis, Queercore's answer to RuPaul, who was interviewed by editor La Bruce while she was fucking him with a strap-on black dildo. I don't know if you can get much queerer than that (and have to thank Canadian journalist Graham Russell for letting me have this information).

In Britain, following the shambolic demise of Riot Grrrl, the new wave of all-girl punk mayhem, Huggy Bear manager Liz Naylor, she of the queer Naylor sisters from Rough Trade, diverted her Cat Call Records to take on Queercore bands like Sister George, the first British Queercore band to release a mini-LP. The *NME* even devoted a spread to Queercore, with bands like The Children's Hour (more lesbian retro?), Parasite and Louisa Trauma. Curiously, however, the majority of the photographs accompanying the feature figured the musicians obscuring their faces. Only The Children's Hour and Spud Jones presented recognizable features.

Queercore is about an attitude more than anything else. It says nothing new – Pansy Division admit their music is a hybrid of post-punk styles, ranging from the Ramones to Billy Bragg. Perhaps what's important here, though, is that before there hadn't *been* queer bands who were influenced by The Ramones and Billy Bragg. Queercore could be dismissed as derivative, but its importance is in its message, which is empowering young fans and musicians who feel ignored and alienated by what queer culture can offer them. They even say – as did the American Homocore manifesto – that you don't even have to be queer to be queercore. It could all disappear overnight. It could be a pose, a gust of hot air, a passing phase. It could also be the most important thing ever to have happened in the history of queer noises.

Chapter eighteen

Is Madonna Queer?

IN 1986, during the dead time between Christmas and New Year, I went on the road around Britain for a few days with the Human League, to write a piece about them. They were playing a short warm-up tour of nightclubs and small halls prior to a national tour in the new year to promote what would turn out to be their last-ever album, *Crash*.

I will die loving the Human League. They were one of the first bands I ever interviewed, when Phil Oakey still had a Veronica Lake hairdo and a day job as a hospital porter in Sheffield. In any of their guises, early or late, the Human League epitomized for me all that can be great in pop music, marrying James Brown to Kraftwerk with a glam-rock wallop. I left the tour after they played Margate's Winter Gardens, one of those seaside venues decorated like the interior of an ocean liner from a Marx Brothers movie. The hall itself was tacky, but when the lights went down the Human League transformed this windy barn into a small and sweaty nightclub pumping with dance music.

I got a lift back to London in a car full of other journalists who had driven down to see the show. Our ears were still ringing from what had been a magnificent set, in particular an electrifying version of 'Seconds', their song about the Kennedy assassination. During the two-hour drive back to London, we talked of all manner of things: trap five journalists in an enclosed space for any length of time and they will dish the A-M telephone directory. One of the journalists, a woman from a glossy magazine for teenagers, recounted her strange experiences on an assignment with a major chart act. She had been assigned to take them nightclubbing for an evening and then write it up for her readers. She knew that these musicians were gay, but closeted, and was slightly surprised when they ended the evening at Heaven. When she asked what they were doing at Heaven, the musicians, obviously a few drinks west of caution, told her, 'Because this is where we get our dick!'

This was not something that her magazine could print, even if she had wanted to, and like most liberal heterosexuals she wasn't about to start her own one-woman outing campaign. She let the comment pass, and they spent an uneventful evening dancing and drinking at Heaven. By the time she arrived at her office the next day, the detour to Heaven wasn't even going to appear in her piece.

The detour to Heaven did, however, feature rather prominently in discussions taking place between the chart act's managers and their record company press office. Soon, the record company's head of press was on the telephone, asking for assurances that the piece wasn't going to be unfavourable towards the chart act. Specifically, they hoped that the piece would contain no mention of the trip to Heaven. The publicist employed the mixed tones of wheedle and threat. The delicate ecology of pop publicity had been upset, and the journalist was expected to restore it to a state of order, even if the only thing that had really had a crimp put in it was the cowardice and paranoia of the major chart act. We might think of this as the Chaos Theory of celebrity: a silly remark in Heaven might quite easily cause terrifying storms on the front page of the *Sun*. Worst of all was the presumption of the record company, which itself was more chaos theory: storms on the front page of the *Sun* might cause sudden slumps in advertising revenue for a glossy magazine for teenagers, the ending of friendly relations between that magazine and the chart act's record company, and this could extend, as happens in chaos theory, unfolding like a Fibonacci series or Mandelbrot set, to affect the magazine's relations with other record companies that had closeted pop stars on their books or closeted gays in their management hierarchy – which, unsurprisingly, means most record companies.

Her ire that night, as we sped through the hop-fields of Kent in the small hours, was reserved for the drunken pop stars, who had woken up the following morning, done something about their hangovers and then told their management and record company to silence her – when she had no intention of exposing her erstwhile companions on the dance-floor at Heaven anyway. That pop stars should behave in this way these days was a story out of Kenneth Anger's *Hollywood Babylon* and was, she felt, both sordid and rather sad. In the late 1980s, when blatant queers topped the charts, it seemed bizarre that these people felt unable to come out. And the fear of personal repercussions – among family and friends – seemed to be far outweighed by commercial concerns, namely the continuing belief that queer acts can't break America, or at least as big as they and their record companies would like them to.

Yet enough brazenly queer performers had stated their sexuality, indeed insisted on it being known, to suggest that a successful career in pop and retaining one's personal dignity and integrity as a self-identified queer were not mutually exclusive. It might well be that the giants of the American music industry – Sony, say, or MTV – would have a covertly homophobic management, but neither would refuse the opportunity to make money out of a successful band or act. The great American public might not fall for you as much as they did for U2 (who, again, dressed up as queers on the cover of *Achtung Baby*, and that didn't seem to harm sales of the album), but not even U2 need to be as rich as U2, which is why they support so many humanitarian charities. If remaining in the closet is the only way a star can be loved in Boise, Idaho, I have to ask, what sort of lunatic wants to be loved in Boise, Idaho, that badly anyway? Either a deranged egomaniac of the calibre of Norma Desmond, or perhaps one other category of individual, someone who really cannot come to terms with the social and political implications of their sexuality.

Furthermore, artists from David Bowie to Madonna have boosted flagging careers by flirting with queer sexuality, and it seems to have been proven time and again that a recognizably queer subtext adds a frisson, a burnish or sheen that appeals to an audience that likes to think itself trendy (and whose *raison d'être* is, in fact, that very quality). Put it another way: in rock's Pearl Harbor of sunken hypes, from Grand Funk Railroad to Sigue Sigue Sputnik, how many failed out gay pop stars can you count? (And no, Jobriath, the lamentable nitwit with the goldfish bowl on his head, does not count.)

The success of Right Said Fred should have been the final nail in the coffin of the closeted pop star syndrome, yet even they played the well-actually-I'm-bi (or out and, er, out straight) card after that first brilliant single and its outrageous video. While Richard Fairbrass has given some outspoken interviews, Right Said Fred are camping it up down at the end of the pier with the majority of queer pop acts, and are supine in the arms of the Fleet Street gossip machine. As a young gay rock fan wrote in a letter to *Vox* magazine, why is it that gay rock fans have to look to heterosexual bands – such as The Senseless Things' 'Homophobic Asshole' and The Lemonheads' 'Big Gay Heart' (and these aren't necessarily wholly het bands, but, again, the poor reader isn't to know that) – for popular music that speaks to their experience? In the case of Tongue Man, why do they have to look to heterosexual critics on 'heterosexual' papers to tell them about this music?

Even Madonna, who has gone the furthest in using explicit queer imagery in pop, has failed to break this impasse. She has spawned a small but thriving industry among post-structuralist academics, male and female, who have deconstructed the material girl until she must be black and blue from the prodding. Her statements and poses certainly chime with the in-your-face antics of queer theory, but at heart she's still a 1970s liberal. Parts of *Sex*, indeed parts of the 'Erotica' video, may overlap with lesbian SM porn, but at the end of the day she's a died-in-the-wool feminist of the old school who has perhaps taken a few pages out of Marlene Dietrich's book and begun to play with her stage and offstage persona.

Where queer joins hands with post-modernism to inaugurate sly and subversive games of meaning, like Jon Savage's polysemiotic defence of punk imagery, revelling in surface, ambiguity, irony and quotation to such an extent that its real meaning – or 'real' 'meaning', as the Madonnaologists would probably insist – is impossible to pin down, Madonna is an old-fashioned content and role-model gal. Interviewed about her quite public celebration of sexuality, about her wealth, about her image and about her career, she talks of giving young women a powerful role-model of a woman in control of her career, her destiny and, as Suzanne Moore has pointed out, her vagina. (Suzanne Moore's description of her, if memory serves, was of a 'voracious clitoris', at least I think it was clitoris.) No subversive games with ambiguity and meaning here, rather a woman using sexual symbolism as a weapon of radical, well, debate would seem too let's-sit-down-and-discuss-it a word for a girl who wants it right now and wants it on its knees and begging. Media intervention might be the best description. (Either way, anyone who can hospitalize Martin Amis with a severe attack of vagina dentata without actually meeting him has to be on the right track.) The same could be said of performers such as Karen Finley, and art terror squads like the Gorilla Girls, who are master-minded at least in part by Laurie Anderson.

Argument still rages among the Madonnaologists, some of whom see her tactics as backing up into the very dead ends (objecti-fication, control, violence) from which feminism has fought to free women. Queer theorists are, to lift a joke from the valedictory statement by a now-defunct lesbian SM group, 'too fucking busy, and vice versa' to care about feminist theory. I am hamstrung by the fact that I can understand the reasoning in both: I learned my sex politics from the former and applaud the radicalism of the latter, and while I would probably defer to the former I am at least glad that this argument is taking place. As Holly Near writes, while gay male culture has seeped into pop over the decades, the same cannot be said of the culture of the women's movement; 'and we were asking more questions than David Bowie was'. It may also eventu-ally be proved, as Burchill and Parsons said, inaccurately, of Tom Robinson, that queer theory is in fact wanking into the wind.

History may well ask whether David Bowie was asking any questions at all, or merely pillaging other people's wardrobes to camouflage his own appropriations from the lexicon of rock'n'roll. David Jones's intentions were purely theatrical, with some crude literary references slapped on to impress heterosexual rock critics like Michael Watts. The political impact was entirely accidental: as Jones told Watts, he had no time for the gay liberation movement, in fact despised it. We queers were too stupid, or too in the thrall of Jones's publicity, to recognize this cynical manipulation: it took two equally cynical heterosexual American writers to point this out, and neither did so out of a sense of affinity with the gay sub-culture. Still, to repeat myself, I and many others have reason to be grateful to the myth of Queer David.

The problem is that the history of queer noises has been one of being grateful, for whatever scraps the dominant culture might grant the queer underground, for whatever few courageous individuals decided to stand up for themselves, and for the encoded forms of music – opera, musicals, disco – that in the most generous reading possible can be said to have sustained the siege mentality that informs so much queer culture. This is not to denigrate those musics – I write as an unreconstructed, if elderly, disco bunny who has seen virtually every London production of Stephen Sondheim's *Sweeney Todd* – simply to say that there has to be life after Sharon Redd.

As I hope this book has shown, there is and always has been life after Sharon Redd, and one that in fact includes and celebrates Sharon Redd, but for a variety of reasons we have not been told about large parts of this music. Certain elites keep this information to themselves; others actively work to censor it or deny its cultural importance; still others want to hide their sexuality, mainly for commercial reasons; some die afraid and are never remembered as the people they really were. I hope this book will offer a basic introduction to the history of this music. I wrote it as an act of reclamation, even of people like Tom Robinson and Bronski Beat, who are in danger of being filed away in the uncertain recording of queer noise history. I also wrote it as a refutation of the heterosexual propaganda – spookily echoed in the editorial policies of some of the gay media – that queers don't make or listen to this music.

We do.

It is important to remember this, to roll back the heterosexual erasure and denial of this history and perhaps surprise a few queers who don't belong to the loathsome elites who control this information. I wrote it as someone who has written about a lot of different musics in the past, simply because my job made me learn about them. So much of this music has meant so much to me in my life, and so much of it is unknown, ignored or even dismissed by the conduits of popular discourse in queer culture. I also wrote it, of course, thinking that the time has come for pop stars to stop skulking around in Heaven and expecting a complacent media to shore up their closets for them.

Knowing that there are other queer fans of Billy Strayhorn

and John Cage, Bessie Smith and Steve Martland, Cecil Taylor and Maggie Nichols, Gary Burton and Tongue Man, who don't get told these things by the self-appointed arbiters of this culture, I am happy to confess also that it was written with the words of the sainted Emma Goldman in mind: I won't join your revolution if I can't dance.

Index